RAISING
Resilient Kids

Raising Resilient Kids
Copyright © 2018 Collective Wisdom Publications
PO Box 150, Mt Evelyn Victoria 3796

First printed August 2018
Updated Edition April 2019

Distributed in Australia by Woodslane Pty Ltd
www.woodslane.com.au

Contributing Authors:
Dr Michael Carr-Gregg
Susan Mclean
Melinda Tankard Reist
Sharon Witt
Michael Grose
Michelle Mitchell
Collett Smart
Hugh van Cuylenberg
Wendy Mason

ISBN 978-0-648 3732-0-9

Cover Design: Bec Matheson www.becmatheson.com
Typesetting and design by Communique Graphics: ivan@cgraphics.com.au
Printed in Australia by Openbook Howden Print & Design
www.openbookhowden.com.au

Edited by Sharon Witt
sharon@sharonwitt.com.au
With special thanks to James Cummings for additional editing
and proof-reading.

Inside

Introduction

Resilience is a term that has gained traction in recent years, becoming the "buzzword" if you will. It's easy to see why. It's a word that resonates with parents, carers, educators – anyone who is involved in the lives of children and teenagers, as we all have similar goals – namely, to develop strong, capable, well-balanced and above all, kind and decent young people.

I'm not sure about you, but as an educator of adolescents for the past twenty-six years, I have found it to be increasingly evident that many of our young people are struggling to develop the mechanisms of resilience that enable them to work through challenges, manage mistakes and perceived failures, and cope with many issues that children have faced for decades. Instead, mental health concerns are consistently on the rise. Our young people are navigating not just their day to day lives, but their online lives simultaneously, and they are growing up in such a hyper-sexualised culture that it is no wonder that body image issues continue to cause great concern.

In the most recent Mission Australia Report (2017) of which 24,000 young people participated, concerns around mental health continue to surface, as well as coping with stress, body image and depression. For the first time since the survey began, 16 years ago, Mental Health was noted as the top national issue among young people.

Many parents seem to be struggling with the basics of raising children, and they are desperate for any guidance or support on offer. However, as a professional who works with children and parents on a regular basis, what I have discovered is that many are operating in survival mode.

Parents are endeavoring to raise resilient children, yet they are floundering under the immense pressures of life, and its myriad physical, emotional and mental health challenges.

Throughout this book, a number of Australia's best experts will touch on some of the biggest and most challenging influences on young people today – including cyber safety, pornography, anxiety and self-harm – and they offer not only current statistics and information, but strategies to help us as parents, educators, youth workers, and carers, to navigate this minefield and raise them to become confident, resilient people.

Some chapters are incredibly confronting.

I know they were difficult for me to read at times, and it can feel like it would be far easier to just bury our heads in our hands and lament that it is all just too difficult.

Imagine for a moment, being a young person growing up today. There is a lot for them to navigate – far more than I believe any of us as parents and educators had to work through when we were young.

Whether your child or teenager is struggling to bounce back from difficult circumstances or personal struggles, or if they are challenged by anxiety or online bullying, my hope is that there might be one or more chapters of this book that will resonate with you and provide not only some guidance, but a sense of hope.

Each of the contributors to this book have been asked to do so because they work with and care very much about our young people. Secondly, they have an expertise in the topic they write about.

We have provided contact details for each of the contributors, should you wish to seek assistance or further information to help you navigate the often difficult role of parent, educator or carer of a young person.

This book is by no means a comprehensive guide to helping young people develop resilience. In fact, for some readers, you may feel more challenged in your role. But I have always been of the belief that to be forewarned is to be armed. And as parents, we don't know what we don't know. This book came out of a deep desire to help parents, educators and anyone who works with young people, to gain an understanding of some of the biggest concerns that affect our children. If you have young children right now, you may be fearful of the environment in which you are raising them. But I want to encourage you. You are doing a great job! And in reading this book, you may be able to provide valuable support and wisdom to a child, teenager, another family or young person in your life.

My deepest thanks to the authors and presenters featured in this book, who so willingly invested in this project, with the sole aim of equipping those working with this generation of children: Dr Michael Carr-Gregg, Susan McLean, Melinda Tankard Reist, Michelle Mitchell, Michael Grose, Collett Smart, Wendy Mason and Hugh van Cuylenburg.

Sharon Witt

RAISING
Resilient Kids

This book is a result of many, many parents and educators asking us to create a resource after the success of our 'Resilient Kids Conference' which began as a seed of an idea, to provide a one-day conference where those who needed encouragement and equipping for their role in children's lives could come along and hear from some of Australia's leading experts.

*We are now taking it nationwide, so if you would like to come to a one-day event and be equipped and inspired in the role that you play in raising children and teens, further information can be found at **www.resilientkidsconference.com.au***

Dr Michael Carr-Gregg

Dr Michael Carr-Gregg is one of Australia's highest profile adolescent and child psychologists. He wrote his PhD at the University of NSW on Adolescents with Cancer and named and founded CanTeen more than 30 years ago with a group of young cancer patients. He has worked as an academic, researcher, and political lobbyist. He is also the author of 14 books and is an Ambassador for Smiling Mind, Big Brothers Big Sister, and sits on the Board of the Family Peace Foundation and the National Centre Against Bullying. He is a columnist for a number of publications, including *The Huffington Post*, *Girlfriend* magazine and the Australian Boarding Schools Association publication *LightsOut*. Michael has been the consultant psychologist for the Australian Boarding Schools Association for over 15 years and is the resident parenting expert on Channel 7's *Sunrise*, psychologist for Channel 9's *Morning Extra*, as well as the *Morning Show* with Neil Mitchell on Radio 3AW. He is married with 2 sons and is a special Patron of the Hawthorn Football Club.

www.michaelcarrgregg.com

@MCG58

How to build happy and resilient children

Between the 7th September and the 11th May 1941, the German Air Force known as the Luftwaffe, bombed London and surrounds for 56 consecutive nights, in a part of the Second World War that became known as the 'Blitz'. More than 40,000 civilians were killed, and over a million homes were destroyed. My father, John Carr-Gregg Snr, aged twenty, was in London during the Blitz and I once asked him what it was like and how he coped. His response was instructive. He said, "Oh, there were signs up everywhere saying *Keep Calm and Carry On*, and we just did." This was clearly a generation who not only managed their incredibly challenging day-to-day lives but also were able to recover from multiple set-backs and adversity – they were resilient.

My father died 5 years ago at the ripe old age of 93, and he rarely ever spoke of the war, as I suspect he was deeply traumatised by it. But I often wonder how this generation of young people would cope with a similar scenario. I suspect not well, and both schools and parents have to accept some of the responsibility.

The seeds of this resilience deficit disorder are sewn early. In kindergarten childhood games like musical chairs and pass the parcel have been changed so no one loses and everyone gets a prize while unwrapping the parcel. Moreover, many of our primary schools have adopted a policy of rewarding children for participation; everyone gets a ribbon or a trophy. Some schools have banned hugging[1], somersaults and cartwheels[2], ball games[3], and even best friends,[4] worried that if the relationships break up, the students would be sad. It is incredible that some adults and teachers are actively strategizing and manipulating children's friendships in a mistaken effort to over-protect them. They're not only risking extinguishing a fundamental part of growing up, but being an adult as well. We are potentially witnessing the gradual 'woozification' of an entire generation.

The irony is that other parts of the education system have placed such an emphasis on educational testing through NAPLAN and the ATAR that we are simultaneously providing this generation with multiple opportunities to fail, without providing them with the skills, knowledge or strategies to manage their failures. The result is the primary school teacher, to whom I spoke last month, who has a bunch of grade 3 students who simply dissolve into tears when they can't do a math problem.

This lack of resilience could explain the apparent rise in the high prevalence of disorders in our young people – particularly depression, anxiety and self-harm – and may be contributing to the fact that our youth suicide rate is the highest in ten years.[5] A new analysis of Victorian emergency departments released in May revealed that mental health presentations in 14 to 19 year olds had tripled between 2008 and 2015, and presentations of self-harm were up 52%.[6] Certainly, a brief perusal of the Mission Australia Annual Youth Survey[7], which takes the psychological temperature of over 24,000 15 to 19-year old's each year – shows there is little room for encouragement. Over the past 5 years the number of young people who were extremely or very concerned about their ability to cope with stress (45.3%) seems to increase each year and may well hit 50% this year.

"One my favourite parenting mantras is to never do anything for your child that they could do for themselves."

Maggie Dent a well-known parenting expert writes, "…we are living in a time when children are less resilient, so by the time they get to adolescence they are floundering in a world that has changed more rapidly than ever. It's tricky out there. We've always had a generation gap but now it's a chasm."[8] One my favourite parenting mantras is to never do anything for your child that they could do for themselves. Unfortunately, many parenting researchers have found that many of today's parents and institutions have done so much for young people when growing up that they have shielded them from any adversity and inadvertently stopped those young people from doing things for themselves.

'Psychological' resilience is defined as an individual's ability to face, overcome, be strengthened by and be transformed by adversity. It is about survivability and bounce-back-ability, to successfully adapt to life tasks in the face of social disadvantage or highly adverse conditions. Such adversity can come in the shape of family or relationship problems, health problems, or workplace and financial worries, among others.

"Resilience is one's ability to bounce back from a negative experience."

Resilience is one's ability to bounce back from a negative experience. Resilience is not a rare ability; in reality, it is found in the average individual and it can be learned and developed by virtually anyone. Resilience should be considered a process, rather than a trait to be had. It is a process of individuation through a structured system with gradual discovery of personal and unique abilities.

A common misconception is that resilient people are free from negative emotions or thoughts and remain optimistic in most or all situations. To the contrary, resilient individuals have, through time, developed proper coping techniques that allow them to effectively and relatively easily navigate around or through crises. In other words, people who demonstrate resilience are people with an optimistic attitude and positive emotionality and are, by practice, able to effectively balance negative emotions with positive ones.

Professor Emmy Werner was one of first early social scientists to use the term 'resilience' in the 1970s. She conducted a study of a cohort in a forty-year longitudinal study[9] of 698 infants on the Hawaiian island of Kauai – the island's entire birth cohort for the year 1955. Kauai was quite poor and many of the children in the study grew up with alcoholic or mentally ill parents. Many of the parents were also out of work. Werner noted that of the children who grew up in these detrimental situations, two-thirds exhibited destructive behaviours in their later teen years, such as chronic unemployment, substance abuse, and out-of-wedlock births (in case of teenage girls). However, one-third of these youngsters did not exhibit destructive behaviours. Werner called the latter group 'resilient'. Thus, resilient children and their families were those who, by definition, demonstrated traits that allowed them to be more successful than non-resilient children and families.

The major traits of resilient children:

Charismatic Adult

In their book, Brooks and Goldstein[10] cite the work of the late author and psychologist, Dr. Julius Segal, in proposing that all children need "charismatic adults" in their lives. Charismatic adults in the lives of children can be parents, but they can also be other significant adults in a child's life and are often teachers. Dr Segal defined the role of the charismatic adult as "a person with whom children identify and from whom they gather strength." According to Brooks and Goldstein, these adults convey love and acceptance and are willing to advocate for a child, especially in times of need.

Positive Self-Talk

Self-talk is basically a person's inner voice, the voice in our mind which says things that we don't necessarily say out loud. Often self-talk happens without people even realising it and can be a subtle running commentary going on in the background of your mind. But what you say in your mind can determine a lot of how you feel about who you are. Positive self-talk is the stuff that makes people feel good about themselves and the things that are going on in their lives. It is like having an optimistic voice in one's head that always looks on the bright side.

Social-emotional Competencies

Social and emotional learning is about learning how to manage feelings and friendships, and solve problems. These are essential life skills that support wellbeing and positive mental health. Social and emotional skills promote children's ability to cope with difficulties and help to prevent mental health problems. Children who have developed social and emotional skills find it easier to manage themselves, relate to others, resolve conflict, and feel positive about themselves and the world around them.

Islands of Competence

This is about finding one's passion or "spark". The idea is that one of the most important tasks for a young person is developing areas of growing skill and competence. Self-esteem really comes from developing capabilities, be that art, music, dance, drama or sport; and in the process, children learn the importance of practice and persistence.

Spirituality

Defined as a sense of connectedness or relatedness to something or someone that transcends the material world is associated with better mental health. It can help increase self-esteem, aid in one's search for meaning in life, improve family and special relationships and decrease risk-taking behaviour. It can also provide a moral compass to help navigate life.

I believe that these factors are useful and should prompt parents and other adult carers to think about their offspring and ask key questions:

- Does your child have a charismatic adult in their life?

- Do they display positive, flexible self-talk?

- Do they have a spark (islands of competence), something that gets them up in the morning?

- Does your child have a sense of connectedness or relatedness to something bigger than themselves?

Maggie Dent calls these charismatic adults 'lighthouses', and she describes them as caring, genuine adults who have a meaningful involvement with a young person and show a willingness to help them navigate the sometimes – rocky terrain of adolescence. So how can you become a 'lighthouse'? Such people are great communicators, give guidance when asked and have a developmental perspective, in that they understand young people, their stages and developmental tasks. They are trustworthy, have the courage to care, dole out encouragement and hope, build connectedness through genuine acceptance, and teach life skills.

> *"...'lighthouses'... caring, genuine adults who have a meaningful involvement with a young person..."*

As far as happiness is concerned, one of the greatest predictors of happiness is your child's ability to obtain, maintain and retain prosocial peers.

Translated from psychobabble, this boils down to the ability of your son or daughter to make good friends. This requires one of Emmy Werner's key components of resilience, namely good social and emotional competencies – the ability to read people and their emotional cues.

Professor Werner's concepts have stood the test of time. More recent and increasingly sophisticated studies of resilience[11] have found a range of different risk and protective factors in the individual, their family, school and friends, which also contribute to the creation of resilient young people. Protective factors, that increase the likelihood of resilient behaviour include intellectual functioning, parenting quality, achievement of developmental milestones, easy temperament, authoritative parenting, and improved verbal and non-verbal ability.

If parents can make sense of some of the components of resilience, then they can and should work to boost, develop and enrich these factors as part of their overall parenting. My two top tips for great millennial parenting are:

"The word 'No'... has fallen out of fashion at many homes, with parents opting for a more friendly, egalitarian approach to raising teenagers."

Give them Vitamin 'N'
They need to hear the word 'No' – No, you cannot watch Netflix all day. No, you may not skip dinner. No, you may not use the car. This word has fallen out of fashion at many homes, with parents opting for a more friendly, egalitarian approach to raising teenagers. Young people are not emotionally or developmentally equipped to make major decisions or rules, or to self-regulate; their brains are still a work in progress. That's your job. And if you don't do it, your child will feel a sense of bewilderment and internal disorder, which could manifest itself in your son or daughter acting out.

Set limits and boundaries
Adolescence is a time of seeking autonomy and pushing the limits. As teenagers break the childhood bonds that bound them to their parents they need assistance to help moderate the rate of change.

Establishing limits over things that matter, (sleep, curfews, alcohol, sex, drugs, exercise and diet) things that relate to their wellbeing, are the means by which parents control the rate of change; helping their sons and daughters find a reasonable and balanced approach to growing up.

* * * * * * *

One thing is for sure, my father John Carr-Gregg Snr and his generation, faced with the death, destruction, nightly bombs, gas masks and rations of the Blitz, truly earnt the name 'The Greatest Generation'. The question remains, how would this generation cope, should the world implode again?

Footnotes:

1. https://www.mamamia.com.au/hugging-ban-is-not-the-way-to-go/
2. https://www.news.com.au/news/outrage-as-school-bans-cartwheels/news-story/b81e6daac1baec8b582610ef3ac12d2e
3. https://www.heraldsun.com.au/leader/outer-east/dorset-primary-school-bans-children-from-bringing-balls-to-school/news-story/c949e74fcdc6254bf1a7ef5cdeaaf312
4. https://honey.nine.com.au/2018/04/23/15/43/mum-furious-after-preschool-bans-best-friends
5. http://www.abc.net.au/news/2016-11-30/system-for-suicide-prevention-rates-highest-10-years/8076780
6. https://www.mja.com.au/journal/2018/208/8/paediatric-mental-and-physical-health-presentations-emergency-departments
7. https://www.missionaustralia.com.au/publications/annual-reports/annual-report-2017
8. Parentsguides.com.au Mental Health 101, p.14
9. Werner, E. E. (1971). The children of Kauai: a longitudinal study from the prenatal period to age ten. Honolulu: University of Hawaii Press, ISBN 0870228609.
10. https://www.springer.com/gp/book/9781461436607
11. https://aifs.gov.au/cfca/publications/resilience-still-useful-concept-when-working-child/what-resilience

Wendy Mason

Wendy Mason is the Director of Early Learning at an Independent School in Melbourne. An early childhood specialist, she leads the development of their early years programs. She has been an educator in early childhood settings, TAFE and Primary school for over 30 years.

Wendy is passionate about developing resilience, social skills, and building a strong sense of wonder and curiosity about the world we live in. She loves connecting children with nature and inspiring sustainability practices. She values the uniqueness of childhood and encourages hands-on learning through exploration, discovery and play.

Wendy is the co-author of the picture storybook series for young children, *When I'm shining with Light*, a part of the Kids Light Up project, which is a forum for educational information with a foundational basis for teaching resilience with specific positive values and qualities.

Wendy is married to Roger, and mother to two adult children.

www.kidslightup.com.au

@KidsLightUp

kidslightup

Future-proofing our children by nurturing resilience

We all want to raise kids who are resourceful, resilient and ready to succeed at school and beyond. Being a resilient child requires a mindset that deeply believes that; I am not the sum of my mistakes, I can try again, things will get better, I am not alone. Raising a resilient child is about laying a deep foundation of inner confidence.

What does resilience in a young child look like? Is it being successful at school? Being kind to others? Having lots of friends? Having the ability to bounce back when affected by problems? It's all of these things and more. Being resilient means that we have inner resources, such as using positive self-talk, or thinking back to how you solved a problem before. It also means that we know how to use external resources, such as asking someone to help.

Raising our children to be resilient means that as they grow they will rely on their ability to navigate the emotional rollercoaster of life, make mistakes and learn from them. This chapter describes 3 common societal influences that essentially block resilience development in early childhood, and gives 5 keys to building and developing resilience throughout childhood.

The dis-ease of being busy

Children are growing up in a tough world and parenting has become increasingly complicated. Children have access to greater information than parents have ever had before. We live in a world where our lives are incredibly busy; we are constantly in a state of *dis-ease*, forever being bombarded with e-mails and text messages that require us to respond – now!

We have less time for leisure, less time for reflection, less time for community, less time to just… *be*. We seem to be on our phone – *All the Time*. And it's not just adults that are busy. In a society where we are consumed with extracurricular activities, children have gymnastics, piano and swimming lessons to attend. Do we love our children so much that we over-schedule them, making them stressed and busy?

> *"We have less time for leisure, less time for reflection, less time for community, less time to just… be."*

Yet, despite all this activity, more children than ever are arriving at school with decreased ability to concentrate, the inability to focus and listen, and difficulty articulating their emotions. Moreover many children also experience decreased physical strength, increased aggression, rise in anxiety, lack of energy, unable to self-regulate and *children not playing* and *having an under-developed imagination!* These heightened concerns in childhood are alarming.

Overprotection vs Opportunity

Society keeps finding new ways to frighten parents and educators who often react with overprotection. Many children have everything done for them, every whim catered to, every desire fulfilled – even protected from themselves!

'Helicopter Parents', a term coined in 1990 by child development researchers Foster Cline and Jim Fay, referred to a parent who hovers over a child in a way that runs counter to the parent's responsibility to raise a child to independence. They display behaviours such as hovering over all that children do, handling any mistakes, and attempting to fix all of the child's problems. These parents carry the school bag for their child, stay outside the classroom window, continue to dress their school child in the morning, and have five different breakfast choices just in case the child changes their preference. Over-protection of children has ramped up in the last few years, such as with the 'lawn mower parent' or 'bulldozer parent', who clear all perceived obstacles out of the child's way. We see teachers increasingly blamed for low grades at school, or misbehaviour explained with excuses.

A good way to describe society's influence on parenting is the changes we've seen in the good old-fashioned party game *Pass the Parcel* – somehow over time this well-loved party game has morphed into everyone getting a prize, no winners or losers, just to make sure no-one is unhappy. The original game had nothing to do with being happy, and everything to do with joyful celebration of others! It's easy to see how children are being robbed of opportunities to learn how to navigate disappointment.

Further evidence of over-protection in society can be noticed at the local early childhood centre or the park where poles and walls are wrapped in a crash mat or soft padding, just in case a child bumps into it. Play equipment at the park has become so predictable that there is no challenge. Children are spending large amounts of time inside. Entertainment is provided for children, rather than them being given the opportunity to use their imagination.

Many children have everything done for them; they have no autonomy, and they are not in control of themselves. Is it any wonder that children in these circumstances are unable to navigate big emotions when the adults around them control all aspects of their life? Even if you're not an over protective parent, teaching your child to navigate peers who do not have these skills can be tricky.

> *"It's easy to see how children are being robbed of opportunities to learn how to navigate disappointment."*

Learning to fail

It seems that we live in an age of fear of either letting children fail or wanting them to fail in order to learn the hard lessons in life. We are less inclined to allow them to fail, fall, have a setback or be disappointed. Somewhere along the line we have softened parenting to the point of thinking that children's normal dispositions to making poor choices are labelled as mistakes. Children push boundaries, they drop things, fall over, struggle to share and scream and shout when they don't get what they want. These are all opportunities for children to build resilience. The trick is helping our children learn to accept mistakes and failure well.

When children are learning to fail, it is important to remember that very young children are egocentric; their sphere of self is very tightly wrapped around them. During a child's early development this self-centeredness circle grows to encompass others, starting with family, then moves to social groups such as sport and church, school, neighbourhood, etc. Early childhood behaviours typically include being uncoordinated, take what one wants when they want it, having difficulty waiting for others or forgiving others when they are wronged. Young children make lots of mess, can be very loud, make demands, and can be very unreasonable. They are also wonderers of the world around them, curious about the tiniest thing, insistent about asking why, create hypotheses and perform science experiments. They persist to achieve their goal when motivated. All of these innate qualities are wonderful! We all need good and bad, strong and weak, frustrating and exciting experiences from which we learn. Experience is a fabulous teacher!

These examples of societal influences on parenting styles are extreme; we have probably all been guilty of some of these things at one time or another. It's not about blaming parents, but becoming aware of these influences and trends, questioning our approaches to nurturing and educating, thinking through tough situations, and asking what will be helpful to our children to learn resilience when things are tough – to use moments and situations as learning opportunities. This often requires us to think in the moment, to be mindful and resilient ourselves against societal expectations.

5 Keys to building resilience in early childhood

Abundance of LOVE

The dreaded childhood tantrum in the middle of the supermarket is a marker in life that leaves us huddled in a corner never wanting to go out again with said child, or it can be an opportunity to sow love and empathy. It takes time, effort and good planning, although even the best-laid plans can go awry! As our child's tension and volume go up, so does ours, naturally. This can be more threatening than the cause of the angst in the first place. It's easy to be fearful of others judging us at these difficult times, and react by applying 'tough love', expecting children to buck up and move on. However, walking away from a child having a meltdown on the supermarket floor hoping they will follow you does not build resilience, it teaches detachment. Same with leaving children to cry themselves to sleep; this teaches detachment, not attachment. A vital link to resilience-building is through loving and trusting relationships.

We want to calm our child down in these moments, get a grip on our own sense of self-control and help them feel they are being heard. Get down at their eye level, make contact, and reflect their feelings back to them in a quiet and calm manner. Loving children unconditionally says things like,

"I won't leave or abandon you, I hear your trouble, there's no rush. When you are ready, we can keep going." It builds resilience that leaves our child with a story of success.

In times of trouble we want to avoid telling children that everything is going to be okay, because often it isn't. Rescuing children isn't helpful in the long run. Inherently, we have an affinity with our child that tells us that when they are in pain, so are we, so much so that above all we want everything to be okay in their world. We must be wary of transferring our concerns onto our child and be aware that children watch

> *"Get down at their eye level, make contact, and reflect their feelings back to them in a quiet and calm manner."*

everything that we do. When a child climbs to the top of a tree, it is natural to want to call out, 'Be careful!'; however, this causes children to doubt themselves rather than assess whether they are safe. It is more beneficial to help children manage their own risk and ask, 'How are you being safe?' It's natural to experience worry, so it's important we communicate that to children. Let's teach our kids that it is good to worry! Society has turned worry into a bad thing, not to be talked about. Worrying is a normal emotion; however, it's important to also teach our kids that just because we are worried about something, it *doesn't mean it's going to happen*. Make it okay to be worried, help them to articulate, 'What am I worried about?' – then think through how to solve the problem, what might the next step be? If it's a worry about having no friends at school, remind them who they have played with before, suggest that we go find that child in the playground before school starts. If your child is worried about not being able to find their classroom, suggest that we go early to school and find it together, then re-trace our footsteps and try to find it again.

Try to help your child let go of *what if...* instead, talk about what we *can* do right now. Teach children to be thought detectives, to catch themselves out when they think negatively, and turn it into a positive thought. Resilience says 'How do I resolve my feelings or problem?' It's about realising that our feelings are real but not necessarily our reality.

> *"Show understanding, and above all, respect. A child learns respect when they experience it."*

Show understanding, and above all, respect. A child learns respect when they experience it. Giving empathy and support goes a long way to show unconditional love. The 'tough love' approach gives children feelings of not being good enough, or that they have somehow failed. Resilience comes through attachment, not detachment, as mentioned earlier. Sometimes we confuse these actions of love with worry of 'spoiling' children, that we are mollycoddling them, wrapping them in bubble wrap. Nevertheless, love is patient and kind, even in the unlovely moments!

Love is the essential ingredient to being human. Enjoy being with your child – build an openness with them that relies on trusting each other and room for talking and listening. Understand that all behaviour is communication, and learning to communicate will take time to learn. Love accepts differences in each other. There is no greater gift that can be offered to our children but our love. It's learned through our actions and reactions, in loving relationship with each other.

Trusting relationships and TIME

Let's counter the *dis-ease* of being too busy and *make* time for important things. So often our busy lives take away opportunities to build resilience. Build family traditions such as family 'All in Night', as there is nothing like sitting around the meal table each night or on a specified evening where conversation is rich and meaningful – back and forth listening and talking using eye contact. It seems such a basic concept but it is so important for language and cognitive development throughout childhood from infancy, babies will benefit from being invited to participate in conversation.

As your family changes, such as when your children bring friends or partners home, the traditions you establish such as family meal times, will stay. No phones or IT devices allowed at the table. Spend quality time, wait for each member to finish eating before leaving the table, have slow conversations that touch on the state of your heart and soul, with expectant pauses and silences that there is no rush to fill.

Social and emotional skills develop through relationship and in relationship with trusted others, such as parents, grandparents, close neighbours, teachers, peers and siblings. Children learn these skills by watching others, and through repetition and practise. From the moment a child is born, they begin to learn these skills through interactions.

Children learn from those around them. They watch when we respond to challenging situations with calmness or anger. They learn to trust adults when they are consistent and stick to what they say – which gives us more reason to think carefully before handing out ultimatums. Choose your battles! Ask yourself – what's really important in this situation? Through trusting relationships children learn to obey. This is such an important skill as they grow, to be discerning about societal rules and make choices to obey for good reasons, such as safety and care for all.

Opportunities to FAIL: to try, and try again

My philosophy in life is to foster an attitude of *'Oh well!'* when things go wrong, or when we make a mistake. *What's the next step?* We demonstrate that we accept that things went wrong but rely on an inner strength to get back to it and try again, to keep going, or to think through the situation and problem-solve. It requires a disposition of persistence through hard times.

One very important thing we can do for our children is to give them emotional literacy – name the emotions they are experiencing and the emotions they see in others. Giving children language helps them process what they are feeling: 'It doesn't seem okay right now, that must really hurt',

'You are feeling angry about losing your ball, and it doesn't seem fair.' Seek the support of picture storybooks, songs and age appropriate shows that all help the specific things that are troubling your child. This will open up opportunities to have meaningful conversations.

We have more emotions than happiness or sadness; we can be angry, tired, frustrated, surprised… the list goes on. Emotions are neither good nor bad; all have significant purpose and meaning. Feelings are real and need to be acknowledged. It's what we do with those emotions that's important. The reaction we have needs to match the incident, given that an incident is minor, such as falling over. Allowing yourself to be comforted, being able to get up, dust yourself off and move on is important. The child is reminded that the 'walking inside rule' is there for a reason. Often a big emotion is followed with a big reaction, 'He took my toy, I'll react with a thump.' This is where language is so important; teach children that using words is more powerful, and if you haven't been heard by your peer/sibling then get an adult to help you.

DOING for themselves

When children have the opportunity to carry their own bag into school, they not only build responsibility for their belongings, they walk into school more grounded. Carrying a heavy bag physically gives sensory feedback; it is heavy work, which can be very calming and settling as children prepare to start their day at school. Sitting in front of a screen before school does the opposite. It switches the brain off, it is passive and addictive. Have you noticed how hard it is to get out of the door on time when the favourite show or game is being watched/played?

"Children love responsibility; it's an opportunity to meet high expectations of themselves, and to experience what it's like to be in the adult world."

Children love responsibility; it's an opportunity to meet high expectations of themselves, and to experience what it's like to be in the adult world. How we think about children is vital, as it influences how we treat children. Do we think that a two-year-old carry the mug to the kitchen? Do we think they are empty vessels ready for us to fill them up with our knowledge? Or do we think that children are already capable, strong learners, having built up knowledge from their innate capabilities and their environment? If we see children as physically and emotionally fragile then our behaviour toward them will reflect this. Always assisting children isn't always helping them. By allowing children to do things for themselves and others gives opportunities to build an 'I can' attitude. It says to the child, 'I believe in you.'

Children's pretend play is a chance to feel what it's like to be grown-up, and their role-play often reflects dramas that they see the adults in their life enacting. 'You be the Mum, and I'll be the baby', or 'I'll be the cat, and you be the dog.' Dramas unfold such as giving birth, being the baddy, going to jail, or being a policeman. Children experience control through this play in a secure way when there is no real power to control what happens to them in their life. Children give each other roles that are monitored through testing out power against each other in a safe environment. These play schemes are important for children to enact, revise and revisit over and over again. They base what they know and try out what they don't know. The 'What if…' scenario is applied, scary developments are played out, helping children to normalise their lives, experience big feelings in a good way, and be okay.

Independent PLAY: GO OUTSIDE

One answer to the rising concerns in early development is to give children what's been missing from their childhood in today's society – independence, responsibility and time to play. When kids get a chance to achieve things on their own, their self-management improves. When kids get practise at problem solving on their own and learning social skills in the time-tested way – such as interacting with peers without constant adult supervision – great things happen. When children spend long periods of time outside with nothing much to do the opportunity for creativity and imagination kicks in. And simply by learning to organise and play a game alongside others increases negotiation and leadership skills.

When children say that they are bored, it does not mean that we need to fill their lives with activities or find them something to do. It means that they have disengaged with what's going on around them. It is vital we allow children to be 'bored' and let them develop their own ideas and imagination. Lots of time to do nothing much in early childhood gives children a multitude of learning opportunities – even better if they are outside in nature, building cubbies, digging in the dirt for mini-beasts, or climbing a tree. Given the time and opportunity, children will naturally find things to do. Children will learn to follow their own interests and fascinations, test themselves and stretch their capabilities.

"Children learn from all experiences, routines, outings and interactions."

The idea that children are only learning when they are in a classroom defies reality. Children learn from all experiences, routines, outings and interactions.

How many kids learn what they are really passionate about in the classroom anyway? School is usually adult-led learning, measured against government-tested standards. This is important, and so is intentional instruction, spontaneous and planned. However, lets balance that with planning for children to have long periods of uninterrupted time to play. Let's do our children a favour and make available the option for free play where they can organise their fun *without adults directing them*. When adults stand back and give children space and time, they will thrive.

Allowing children to partake in a combination of moderate and vigorous activities for at least 60 minutes every day – gives better balance, movement and coordination skills, helps develop friendships, improves sleeping habits, increases cooperation, builds teamwork and leadership skills, increases confidence and happiness, reduces anxiety and stress and improves concentration. That's a lot of learning and life skills!

At the end of the day, you are the parent, the caregiver, or the educator. You get to be the expert on your child. It's your discernment about societal pressures that matters. You hold the privilege to shape children to be resilient and help them future-proof themselves.

Susan McLean

Susan is Australia's leading expert in the area of cyber safety and was a member of Victoria Police for 27 years. She was the first Victoria Police officer appointed to a position involving cyber safety and young people, where she established and managed the Victoria Police Cyber Safety Project. She has completed advanced training in the USA in 2007, 2012 & 2015 including the Protecting Children Online Certificate from Fox Valley Technical College, and has successfully completed the 'University Certificate in Child Safety on the Internet' from the University of Central Lancashire, United Kingdom, as well as other international qualifications.

Susan is the commentator of choice for all Australian media and is sought after for her in-depth knowledge and balanced commentary. She collaborates with a variety of international bodies and is a member of the Federal Government's. Online Safety Consultative Working Group. Susan provides regular pro bono advice and assistance to Australian families and schools in relation to online issues and she is often a conduit between a victim of online abuse (and their families) and Law Enforcement to ensure criminal activity is reported and investigated.

Susan works with elite sports such as the AFL, Cricket Australia, Netball Vic as well as Government agencies, corporations, and both medical and mental health clinicians. She also works closely with the main social media sites and is listed on the newly launched Facebook safety resource centre as a trusted expert in the field. Susan is a published author, her book *Sexts Texts and Selfies* (Penguin) is a definitive online safety resource for all those who work with young people.

www.cybersafetysolutions.com.au

Susan Mclean – Cyber Safety Expert

@TheCybercop1

Building resilience in the digital space

The internet and digital technologies are now a permanent feature in our lives and those of our young people. We cannot ignore this fact or attempt to dismiss the internet as a passing fad or fashion. Young people today have been born into a world where they are immersed in technology and subsequently, as parents, educators, and carers, it is vital that we have the knowledge and ability to guide them and help them build resilience and wisdom in the digital space. If you are a parent in the 21st century, this requires parenting in both the digital world and real world. Young people move seamlessly between their online and offline worlds; thus parents must seamlessly parent between them as well.

Young people today have access to and are accessible by millions of people worldwide. This of course, adds an element of risk to all online communication. There seems to be a never-ending array of websites, applications (apps) and online-games that are present in the digital landscape, providing a fertile place for those who wish to harm young people, the perfect opportunity to do so. Children and adolescents are often not aware that their words and photos, which may have been intended for a small audience, sometimes find their way to a larger one, often with both the unexpected and undesirable consequences. Smart devices and social media sites have become part of our children's lives and they strongly influence how our children create, share and exchange information with others. As adults, we need to be there as well, guiding and advising, even if there is some resistance. As parents, that is our job. We cannot simply be casual observers in this space, we must be present.

It sometimes seems an insurmountable task to be up to date with everything we need to know about the online world, but in this chapter, I hope to provide the basics – the four most important things we need to know about keeping our young people safe in the digital space.

Cyber bullying

Cyber bullying is a *way of delivering covert psychological bullying*:

> "It uses information and communication technologies to support deliberate, repeated and hostile behaviour, by an individual or group, that is intended to harm others." (Bill Belsey 2007)

Cyber bullying can be described as any repeated harassment, insults and humiliation that occurs through electronic mediums, such as email, mobile phones and devices, social networking sites, instant messaging programs, chat rooms, web-sites and through participation in online games. Cyber bullying usually occurs between people that are known to each other such as students at school, members of a sporting club, someone from the same social circle or a friend of a friend – at the very least someone you know of. Cyber bullies usually don't drop from cyberspace and attach themselves to a young person. It is however, different when we see an individual attacked online from a large number of different people. This is often called 'trolling'.

"Cyber bullies usually don't drop from cyberspace and attach themselves to a young person"

Cyber bullying is pervasive in nature, incessant, ongoing and can occur 24/7. It is different from bullying in the real world as by virtue of technology the bully can follow a young person into their home and private space. It often occurs with the perception of anonymity i.e. an account in a fake name or a blocked number; however, in many cases, it is clear who is behind the bullying. Like any form of bullying, cyber bullying can be psychologically damaging; which is often more challenging for parents and carers to identify and subsequently act upon. It is often more difficult to identify mental anguish than a physical bruise on a leg, so be aware of any subtle changes in a young person's demeanour or behaviour and investigate accordingly.

Cyber bullying is also very publicly humiliating, as many others can observe what is written or posted online. Even if the perpetrator deletes the initial message/comment etc., it is almost impossible to remove all traces. Young people will often read, and re-read comments multiple times, further causing themselves distress. We know that cyber bullying can and does contribute to poor mental health. Poor mental health can of course lead to tragic consequences. My best advice is – become the world's best expert on your own child and investigate if you are concerned.

What to do if your child has been cyber bullied:

- Thank your child for coming to you – it is a big deal.

- Ask to see what has happened (keep screenshots or print out evidence).

- Reassure them you will help.

- Help them block the person on their device and on the site.

- Report the abuse to the site (report the account and/or the post).

- Enlist the help of the eSafety Commissioner www.esafety.gov.au if the social media site fails to remove the content.

- Inform the school (or sporting club etc.) and leave it in their hands (They legally MUST deal with it as per their cyber bullying policy).

- Check in with your child to see that it has been resolved (act if it has not).

Most school-based cyber bullying is successfully resolved by following the above. Please note that schools are legally responsibility to deal with ALL forms of bullying, including cyber bullying, that is reported, regardless of where and when it occurs. If despite the above, the cyber bullying does not cease, do not hesitate to inform the Police. Cyber bullying is a criminal offence in every State and Territory of Australia.

Sexting

The sending and receiving of naked images is not new. This may be a shock to many parents reading this right now! As soon as phones had a camera device included, people began to use them to send sexy snaps. Whilst as a consenting adult, there is no criminality in this, for young people, they need to navigate both the social and emotional fallout of sharing these images and also the harsh reality that in every State and Territory in Australia other than Victoria, this behaviour constitutes criminal behaviour. Young people don't use the term 'sexting'; its considered an adult term (it's in the Oxford dictionary) but prefer the following:

> Nude
>
> Naked Selfie
>
> Dick Pic
>
> Tit Pic

"Young people don't use the term 'sexting', its considered an adult term..."

'Sexting' is the act of sending sexually explicit or naked messages or photos electronically, primarily between mobile devices, but can include internet applications such as Instagram, Kik, Snapchat, email, or social networking sites.

The issue of these naked pics usually falls into one of the following:

1. Young people being tricked into sending a picture to an online predator (which they are mostly unaware of at the time).

2. Young people tricked into sending a nude to an 'online friend' (predator) and are blackmailed.

3. Young people wanting to impress a potential boyfriend/girlfriend i.e. flirting.

4. Young people sharing the images with someone they are in a relationship with and whom they trust.

A vital part of any conversation with a young person around the taking and sharing of nudes is to explain that it is a criminal offence in every State and Territory of Australia other than Victoria, to take, possess or transmit (share via technology) a naked image of a young person (under the age of 18 years). Victoria has amended its laws so that in certain situations, the Police can deal with the young person in an educative way rather than lay charges. It does not matter how someone came to possess the image, or if you willingly took the photo yourself and sent it on. It is still an offence.

Important information young people must know!

- they cannot give themselves permission to break the law, (take pictures of themselves naked or in a sexually explicit way);

- they cannot give another person permission to break the law (tell another person that they are fine with it); and

- another person cannot give them permission to break the law (Someone telling them that it is okay). Exceptions are of course if a young person has been tricked, threatened or coerced into sending these images – then they are treated as the victim.

Whilst we should not be criminalising young people who are not behaving with criminal intent, the reality is, our laws have not kept pace with technology and how that technology is being used. State laws in Australia define a child as being under the age of 18 years, except for South Australia where the definition is 16 years. Commonwealth Law defines a child for this purpose as under 18 years.

What to do if you find these images of your child or suspect them of being involved?

- Breathe! Don't yell, scream or panic. Try to remain calm. It is really important to be able to speak rationally to your child at this time.

- Talk to them about your concerns or suspicions and allow them time to respond.

- Try to work out how/when this has occurred and who else may be involved. Where are the images now and who may have possession of them? What were the circumstances? Who were they sent to? Have they been forwarded? Are they pics or video (webcam/Skype)? Gather as much information as possible as quickly as possible.

"It is really important to be able to speak rationally to your child at this time."

- Make an appointment to speak to someone at your child's school, if applicable (Counsellor, Home Room teacher, Principal) and inform them of what has occurred. This is important so that the school can support your child as required. If they are not made aware, they can't always guess what is wrong. Also, if the images are being circulated within the school, the appropriate school authorities will need to be involved.

- Be aware that in some instances, Police may need to be involved and schools do have certain legal obligations in relation to the reporting of incidents. Please don't **NOT** tell the school because you are concerned about Police involvement. Police are best placed to deal with these situations and have tools to minimise the impact. Police also have the ability to retrieve data and trace electronic communication. The important thing is to act as soon as you are aware, and if you feel that it is beyond manageable. If your child is the victim of **Image Based Abuse** (IBA) please report to via www.esafety.gov.au for more help and advice.

- Consider other services such a GP for referral to an adolescent psychologist. Some young people are particularly resilient and are able to move on from these situations quickly once dealt with, others aren't. Trust your instincts and if your child's demeanour is changing for the worse; act!

- If you believe that the 'sexting' is a result of your child being 'groomed' online rather than adolescent naivety, please immediately report to your local Police station.

Grooming

The grooming of children is not new; however, the internet offers predators easy and often unfettered access to young people through a variety of apps, games and sites. Any app, game, site or platform that allows one person to communicate with another person will most likely have predators on it. The sites with limited security and those popular with children are those predators will flock to. If it's popular with children, it will be popular with predators. Do not be under the illusion that all children's games with cute cartoon characters are safe. Predators are clever and despite the great job Police do, they cannot arrest their way out. We must educate to prevent; to take away the opportunity by ensuring that young people are making safe decisions online.

Online grooming can be defined as behaviour conducted in a similar fashion to offline grooming, where an adult, through words and actions attempts to loosen a child's inhibitions in relation to sexual content with the aim to share sexual images and/or meet in person.

"Predators ... are sickly sweet, convincing, conniving, and clever."

Online predators take advantage of the natural vulnerabilities of children and adolescents, such as their desire to appear adult, their need for attention, their wanting to please and not make people angry. Children assume that predators will come across as 'mean' and/or 'scary', but it is far from that; they are sickly sweet, convincing, conniving, and clever. They know exactly how to engage with a young person and quickly work to gain their trust.

Tips to minimise the risk of grooming

- Have clear rules about where your child goes online and what they are accessing.

- Keep devices out of bedrooms and bathrooms (naked images/videos are NOT taken in front of mum and dad!

- Know exactly where your child/young person is online just as you would in the real world.

- Talk early and talk often about personal safety – don't talk to people online you don't know in real life.

- Ensure that if your child is playing online games – no headphones, therefore the voices come out of the TV and you can hear.

- Regularly check all contact/games/message/chat lists. Remove anyone who your child does not know in real life.

If you believe your child/teenager has been groomed

- Save and print out all evidence.

- Log off and walk away.

- Do not engage with the suspect.

- Do not report the account to the site (It is easier to get evidence out of open accounts).

- Do not close your child's account (this is a natural reaction, but Police often take over the account to keep the grooming going).

- Visit your local Police station with all your evidence and make a report.

Problematic Gaming – Internet

The issue of problematic internet use or problematic gaming is very, very real. It is also a very divisive topic with some of the view that problematic gaming is a significant issue and those who see it as a total beat-up. The truth however sits somewhere in between. An online game becomes a problem when it **has a negative impact on a person's life or that of their family.** Often, the person playing the game is so engrossed that they are completely unaware of the issue. At its worst, playing online games can take over a person's life to the exclusion of all else. Anecdotally, boys and young men are the most vulnerable to developing online gaming issues. Girls tend to not to want to log off social networking sites; they want to be connected 24/7 and have FOMO (fear of missing out.) Young males, though, have a clearly defined problem with logging off gaming sites, some becoming agitated and violent, demonstrating signs of clinical withdrawal symptoms when finally disconnected.

There is much dialogue and research about which games are the most addictive and unfortunately, there is no easy answer. Any game can become a problem when it has a negative impact on a person. Online games are cleverly designed to target receptors in the brain; they often work on intermittent reward so that a person feels the need to keep playing as they are not sure when they are going to receive the next bonus. Many games also punish a player if they log off before they want you to. For example, your score is reverted to where you started from if you haven't reached a so-called, 'safe point'. No one wants to play for an hour only to

"Any game can become a problem when it has a negative impact on a person."

find all the gains made amount to nothing. They also often connect people with other gamers or perhaps play in a team which means a player feels they must remain playing and involved. It is vital that parents and carers are aware of the content of any game and that it is suitable for the age of the child.

Dr Richard Graham, a psychiatrist and Internet addiction expert at the relationship counselling Tavistock Centre in London, said, 'Some of my clients will discuss playing games for 14, 16 hours a day at times, without breaks, without attending to their physical needs… For those, the consequences are potentially severe.'

"It is vital that parents and carers are aware of the content of any game..."

To assist parents and those who care for children, Dr Philip Tam, an Australian adolescent psychiatrist and an expert in problematic internet use, has developed the 'i.m.p.r.o.v.e' self-assessment tool, which can be used to assess Internet usage in order to find out if Internet use is a problem and what treatment options should be considered. The diagnostic tool can be downloaded from the website www. niira.org.au and used by the young person themselves (for older teens), or by a parent/carer.

The four levels of pathological Internet use (PIU) are:

- Level I – mild impact/early problems.
- level 2 – increased impact/social circle notices (school, peers).
- Level 3 – clinical impact, specific interventions indicated.
- Level 4 – addiction or PIU, major or whole social world impacted.

The corresponding treatment options for each level of PIU are:

- Level I – self-help, parental assistance, managing it at home.
- level 2 – associates, school counsellor.
- Level 3 – GP, clinical psychologist.
- level 4 – psychiatric/inpatient plus medication considerations.

Remember, young people often rebel against parents, but a different person saying the same thing can work wonders. If you are worried, trust your instincts and seek professional assistance.

"The fact is that some online games can be both amazingly positive and devastatingly negative at same time."

And finally, we must not overlook the many positive outcomes that children derive from playing online games. Through games, young people can develop the ability to problem solve, improve and develop motor skills, learn to care for others, learn responsible behaviour and how to work as part of a team. They can also learn coding and other important technological skills that may be of benefit to them in the future. On the other hand, the negatives are real, and parents need to be aware of all the possible outcomes that come with a child playing online games. The fact is that some online games can be both amazingly positive and devastatingly negative at same time.

My top ten tips

1. Remove devices from bedrooms. (This means parents too, unless you have an on-call occupation. Let your kids see that you too can sleep without the phone next to the bed.)

2. Follow the rules of the site. Read the Terms and Conditions of Use and ensure that your child is following them, especially around age restrictions. Don't help your child lie online!

3. Have a family online contract – what are the expectations around safe and responsible technology use?

4. Know your child(rens)'s passcodes and passwords.
   This is not an invasion of privacy – it is PARENTING.

5. Be an active participant in your child's online world.
   Play and explore together.

6. Use Filters.

7. Learn to say NO!

8. Know what sites, apps and games they are using and use them as well.

9. Ensure your child is only talking/engaging with people they know IRL (in real life).

10. Know where your child is in the online world, the same as in the real world.

Helpful Resources:

Sexts Texts and Selfies – How to keep your child safe in the digital space
(Susan McLean, Penguin)

www.cybersafetysolutions.com.au

www.esafety.gov.au

www.aftab.com

www.antibullyingpro.com

www.ceop.gov.uk

www.saferinternet.org.uk

www.netsafe.org.nz

www.ncab.org.au

Melinda Tankard Reist

Melinda Tankard Reist is an author, speaker, media commentator, blogger and advocate for young people. She is best known for her work addressing sexualisation, objectification, harms of pornography, sexual exploitation, trafficking and violence against women. Melinda is the author/editor of five books, including *Getting Real: Challenging the Sexualisation of Girls* (Spinifex Press, 2009), now in its 9th printing, *Big Porn Inc: Exposing the harms of the global pornography industry* (Spinifex Press, 2011, co-edited with Dr Abigail Bray) and her latest release (Spinifex Press, co-edited with Dr Caroline Norma) *Prostitution Narratives: Stories of survival in the sex trade*.

An opinion writer, Melinda is also a regular on morning television and has appeared on ABC's *Q&A* and *The Gruen Sessions,* as well as many other TV and radio programs.

Melinda is co-founder of the grassroots campaigning movement, Collective Shout: for a world free of sexploitation, exposing corporations, advertisers and marketers who objectify women and sexualise girls to sell products and services. An ambassador for World Vision Australia, Compassion Australia, HagarNZ and the youth mentoring body, the Raise Foundation, Melinda is named in the Who's Who of Australian Women and the World Who's Who of Women. She has recently been appointed Senior Lecturer in the Centre for Culture and Ethics, Notre Dame University, Sydney.

www.melindatankardreist.com
www.collectiveshout.org

Melinda Tankard Reist
Collective Shout

@MelTankardReist
@CollectiveShout

Building your child's resilience to pornography

I've just addressed three hundred parents at a school and they are now milling around the coffee table. A woman approaches me, and I know by the look on her face that she is about to tell me something confronting. I'm right. Her seven-year-old son was encouraged, by a slightly older boy, to look up a 'funny website' about his favourite cartoon character, *Shrek.* The little boy did so and was shocked to see the animated green ogre depicted as engaging in violent sexual acts with small boys.

The same week another mother tells me her son was playing an innocent and very popular online children's game when a 'pop up' appeared on the screen depicting hard core sex acts.

A father shares, with tears in his eyes, how his 14-year-old daughter discovered her social media accounts had been hacked, and messages offering herself sexually to boys shared widely in her name.

> *"...six under-age high school girls tell me of constant demands from boys for naked selfies"*

Another distressed mum emails to tell me her six-year-old daughter was repeatedly groped by boys in her primary school.

A few days later, six under-age high school girls tell me of constant demands from boys for naked selfies.

Harming children's sexual templates

Everywhere I go I hear stories like this: Of children using sexual language. Playing 'sex games' in the school yard. Pressuring girls for sexual favours. Being tricked into looking at porn on another child's device. Distressed by explicit images they came across online while searching an innocent term.

Exposure to porn 'pop ups' on sites featuring their favourite cartoon characters or while playing online games is an increasingly common entrée to porn material. To appropriate the loved characters of pre-school and primary school children and turn them into creepy and scary sexual predators is surely an act of callous disregard for the wellbeing of youngsters. Just recently, I came across this headline: "Roblox 'gang rape' shocks mother", which reported a US mum describing her shock at seeing her daughter's female character, on the multiplayer game marketed at children 7+, being sexually attacked by two male avatars.[2]

"This generation of children are guinea pigs in a never-before-seen experiment on their sexual development."

Says writer James Bridle in a post titled *Something is Wrong on the Internet*, "What we're talking about is very young children, effectively from birth, being deliberately targeted with content which will traumatise and disturb them, via networks which are extremely vulnerable to exactly this form of abuse."[3]

This generation of children are guinea pigs in a never-before-seen experiment on their sexual development. With average age of first exposure at eleven, children are discovering pornography before they have even had their first kiss. Their sexual templates are being shaped by violent pornographic acts which are a mere click away – even promoted on some school buses.[4]

How will they will be able to form healthy respect-based relationships in future when pornography is their formative environment?

Educators, child welfare groups, mental health bodies, medicos and parents are struggling to deal with the proliferation of hypersexualised imagery and its impacts on the most vulnerable – children whose sexuality is still under construction.

It starts early, and it's everywhere. The principal of a Catholic primary school showed me an image created by a group of five-year-old boys in class using the PicCollage app. They had been given an in-class assignment to make pictures of their favourite things. These little boys presented their image of two semi-naked women in provocative poses – one had superimposed his face between the women's bodies at breast height.[5]

Listen to Jamie's experience. He was 13 when sucked into porn's dark tunnel.

> *"At first I found it a bit scary and a bit yucky…I didn't know it was possible for people to do those sort of things – and there were lots of nasty close-ups. But it gave me funny feelings and the pictures started to stick in my head… the websites led me to other websites and soon I was looking at ever weirder stuff I could never have imagined – animals, children, stabbing and strangling. I stopped leaving the room and seeing my friends because when I was away from the pornography I was dying to get back to see what else I could find."[6]*

Children like Jamie are seeing and having their sexual arousal conditioned by depictions of extreme cruelty and assault.

Porn as a code of conduct

Through exposure to pornography, our children are receiving distorted ideas about bodies, sex and relationships. They are being taught a code of conduct that includes sexual bullying and harassment, entitlement and dangerous sex acts as normal. One boy asked: "If I have a girlfriend, do I need to strangle her when I have sex with her?"[7]

Over the past decade we have seen a growing trend of younger children engaging in problematic sexual and sexually abusive behaviours generally aimed at younger children – children sexually assaulting children. Child on child sexual assault has quadrupled in Australia and more children than ever before are in specialist treatment programs to address problematic sexual behaviour.[8]

"Through exposure to pornography, our children are receiving distorted ideas about bodies, sex and relationships."

The late Emeritus Professor Freda Briggs AO warned that online pornography was turning children into copycat sexual predators. In her submission to the 2016 Senate inquiry into the harm being done to Australian children through access to pornography on the internet, she drew clear links between pornography and child sex abuse.[9]

Professor Briggs cited a distressing litany of attacks on children by classmates, including a four-year-old boy requiring a chaperone to stop him assaulting other children in 'sex games' at a South Australian kindergarten, a six-year-old boy who forced oral sex on kindergarten boys in the school cubby house and a group of boys who followed a five-year-old girl into the toilets, held her down and urinated on her.

Disturbing research on porn's impact

Teen use of internet pornography is linked to changes in attitudes, including viewing women as "sexual playthings eager to fulfil male sexual desires" according to a recent study. Adolescents who had used violent pornography were six times more likely to be sexually aggressive than those who didn't.[10]

"There is an association between younger age of exposure and poor mental health in later life."

The UK Independent Parliamentary Inquiry into Online Child Protection 2012 found that exposure to porn has a negative impact on children's attitudes to sex, relationships and body image:[11]

"We also found compelling evidence that too many boys believe that they have an absolute entitlement to sex at any time, in any place and with whomever they wish. Equally worryingly we heard that too often girls feel they have no alternative but to submit to boys' demands, regardless of their own wishes".

At a time when young people are experiencing high levels of depression and anxiety, pornography use has been associated with depressive symptoms in daily users. There is an association between younger age of exposure and poor mental health in later life.[12]

Porn's grooming of girls

Through porn, our young people learn that 'anyone will do' as a sex partner, that there should be no emotional connection during sex, that women like to be degraded during sex, that women and girls exist as sexual playthings. That there are no boundaries – and if there are, they should be violated. And when it's all over you just move on.[13]

From my work with thousands of girls around Australia, I have learned that girls feel pressured to adopt pornified roles and behaviours, to provide porn-inspired acts, and to put up with things they don't enjoy. One of the most common questions I am fielding these days is, "How do I say no without hurting his feelings?"

As a 'Plan Australia/Our Watch' report found, girls are tired of being pressured for images they don't want to send, but they seem resigned to how normal the practice has become.[14] Boys use the images as a form of currency, to swap and share and to use to humiliate girls publicly. Girls are putting up with demeaning and disrespectful behaviours, and thereby internalising pornography's messages about their submissive role.

Porn has also contributed to body image dissatisfaction. Boys think they need bigger penises. Girls have their pubic hair removed because boys who regularly consume porn think it is disgusting. Girls who don't undergo porn-inspired Brazilian waxing are often considered ugly or ungroomed by boys as well as by other girls. Genital surgery is on the rise in teenage girls. Girls describe being ranked at school on their bodies compared to the bodies of porn stars. They know they can't compete, but that doesn't stop them thinking they have to. Requests for labiaplasty have tripled in a little over a decade among young women aged 15-24.[15]

Helping our children navigate a sexed-up world

We cannot leave the sexual formation of our young people in the hands of the profit-driven global sex industry. As parents, teachers and other caregivers, we have the passion and influence to offer a counter-attack of education and role-modelling. We need to help our young people critically analyse porn's messages, resist porn culture and seek relationships based on respect and authentic human connection.

So, how do we talk to our young people about pornography, and when?

Introducing the conversation

There shouldn't be just one 'talk'. This is a conversation to be having with your children over many years, at varying stages and as different opportunities arise. Communicating your values early and building a warm and close relationship from the start will make all that follows easier.

Constructive conversations about pornography are:

- age-appropriate,
- pre-emptive and positive
- repeated over many years
- focused on the benefits of relationship-based sexuality[16]

- Be prepared. Read books and websites on the subject (including those sourced below). Talk to other parents who share the same values you hold for your child. Discuss with trusted professionals. Think about what it is you would like to communicate to your child, and also be ready to listen attentively and non-judgementally.

- Make a private, unpressured time and place to talk. Initiating the conversation may feel awkward, but for your child's sake, it has to happen.

- Life presents some great springboards for a talk about pornography. If you see an advertisement, movie, or music video-clip with sexualised imagery, it is an opportunity for discussion. Ask your child what they think about it, and help the conversation move to a discussion of media and its influence our feelings about bodies, relationships, dignity and worth etc.

- Talk about an incident from your own life or someone else's. Anecdotes are a great conversation starter.

- Discuss some situations they might face. What are some creative ways to deal with this? For example, if friends of your young person want to watch porn, your child can ignore it, use humour to escape the situation, explain directly why they don't want to be involved, or make an excuse to leave. They can practice some responses with you so they are ready.

- Your children need to know that you have their back on this. Let them know it is never okay to pressure someone to do anything sexual and this includes watching porn. They should also know it is also illegal to show porn to anyone under 18. Establish an exit strategy for difficult situations. For example, if they text you a single "X", or some other agreed code, they know you will come and pick them up from wherever they are immediately, no questions asked.

- When your child requests access to a device, this is another good time to ask how they will use it. Talk about risks and benefits and your expectations – for example, around supervision, privacy and safety. Consider a written agreement on how they will use their devices and internet access (See Susan McLean's chapter for further helpful suggestions here).

> *"Consider a written agreement on how they will use their devices and internet access."*

- Apply internet filtering software to all home computers, laptops, iPads and phones. Look into kid-safe search engines like Google Kiddle.

- Know what your child is viewing on any kind of screen or internet-enabled device, including YouTube, Netflix, social media, and music videos, as children can be exposed to porn through all these platforms.[17]

- Good screen rules and habits: keep doors open, no devices available when sleeping, use devices only in public rooms. Parents must be able to check social media and internet search history. Keep an eye out for hidden apps on phones.[18]

What if your child/teen has seen pornography?

- Pause. Breathe. Remain calm; anger and shock on your part will increase your child's sense of shame. A 'shame and blame' approach will only make things worse. Give yourself time to settle before responding. Your child hasn't done anything wrong, but the porn industry certainly has. Reserve your anger for **it!**

- Plan time to talk. This is an opportunity to have an important discussion and to connect with your young person in their time of need. This is your chance to protect and empower your child.

- When ready, explain that seeing 'bad pictures' is very common but also very harmful. If you discover something on their phone or laptop/family computer, tell them what you saw. If they have voluntarily revealed it, ask them to describe it. What were they doing at the time? Who were they with? Was it accidental or deliberate? Was there an online chat? Who showed it to them? This should not be an interrogation, but rather a conversation where you are trying to get more information to help and guide your child.

- Ask them how they felt about it, and how are they feeling now?
  Talk about common feelings about porn – curious, fascinated, excited, guilty, uncomfortable, worried, distressed, disgusted, or all at the same time.
  Be sure they know that they cannot control their own gut responses.

- Practical action will now include ensuring there is security and filtering software on all devices, and regularly monitoring online activity (to ensure your child's wellbeing, not as a punishment or because of lack of trust) and your child's mood. If porn was accessed through school or on another child's device at school, alert staff. They have a duty of care to protect children from this material.

- Get professional help if use has become compulsive or if your child is anxious or distressed. Your GP will be able to recommend an appropriate psychologist or counsellor. Other avenues include school counsellors, mental health services, or online.[19] There are people who will help, so keep looking until you find the right person.

- Explore resources to help your child: counselling, books, camps, rites of passage programs, websites etc. I highly recommend two new books 'How to talk to your children about pornography' and 'Good Pictures, Bad Pictures', which are available through my website.[20]

- Look at strategies to increase resilience in your child. This book is a great start. Get outdoors. Spend time with them. Encourage them to take up healthy activities and engage in causes that they care about. This will help them feel good about themselves and act as a buffer between them and harmful cultural messaging.

- Give the power to your child! Pornography is a big problem, but they can be part of the solution. They can be rebels against the system, refusing to fall for the porn industry's counterfeit sexuality. Help kids understand sexuality as emotional, psychological and social qualities, and that pornography will never show them what healthy relationships look like and will hijack good relationships in future.

- Get involved in the movement for cultural change! Of course, I have to say: sign up to **Collective Shout: for a world free of sexploitation**, a growing movement of concerned individuals pressing for change to our hyper-sexualised world – for the sake of our young people and for all of us.[21]

Footnotes;

1. Gelblum B (2017). What is Elsagate? The disturbing videos masquerading as children's favourites on YouTube Kids. The London Economic November 11. https://www.thelondoneconomic.com/news/elsagate-disturbing-videos-masquerading-childrens-favourites-youtube-kids/11/11/

2. BBC News, 3 July 2018 https://www.bbc.com/news/technology-44697788?ns_mchannel=social&ns_campaign=bbcnews&ocid=socialflow_facebook&ns_source=facebook

3. Bridle J (2017). Something is wrong on the internet. Medium November 7. <https://medium.com/@jamesbridle/something-is-wrong-on-the-internet-c39c471271d2>

4. Roper C (2017). Pornographic websites advertised on buses, the State Government profits. Collective Shout May 4, <https://www.collectiveshout.org/pornographic_websites_advertised_on_buses_the_state_government_profits> and Chung F (2017). Brisbane Sexpo ads running on school buses, billboards. News.com 26th June, <https://www.news.com.au/finance/business/media/brisbane-sexpo-ads-running-on-school-buses-billboards/news-story/a8a5b1520d387c7513d4f8b4071f34c9>

5. Tankard Reist M (2016). Early sexualization and pornography exposure: the detrimental impacts on children. Australian Childhood Foundation Prosody Blog <http://www.childhoodtrauma.org.au/2016/july/melinda-tankard-reist>

6. Daily Mail (2012). Online porn warped my brain at 13. April 26. https://www.dailytelegraph.com.au/online-porn-warped-my-brain/news-story/44fa90dc254db37863b7c45dbb9e6a22?sv=8606586615cb17140f35ed359a71e9b9

7. Elgot J (2016). Teach children about pornography before puberty, says Labour. The Guardian Tuesday 1st November. < https://www.theguardian.com/education/2016/nov/01/teach-children-about-pornography-before-puberty-says-labour>

8. Etheredge L and Lemon J (2015). Submission to the Royal Commission into Family Violence 2015: Pornography, problem sexual behaviour and sibling on sibling sexual violence. <http://www.rcfv.com.au/getattachment/B8A6174A-6C6F-495F-BF7B-9CA9BF902840/Etheredge,-Linette>

9. Briggs F (2016). Submission for the Inquiry into the harm being done to Australian children through access to pornography on the internet. Submission 2 available for download at the Committee website <https://www.aph.gov.au/Parliamentary_Business/Committees/Senate/Environment_and_Communications/Online_access_to_porn/Submissions>

10. Owens EW, Behun RJ, Manning JC and Reid RC (2012). The impact of internet pornography on adolescents: a review of the research. Sexual Addiction and Compulsivity 19(1-2):99-122. See also: Tankard Reist M (2018). 'Never Again? Addressing Sexual Violence Must Include Pornography', ABC Religion & Ethics, July 3. http://www.abc.net.au/religion/articles/2018/07/03/4865737.htm

11. UK Parliament (2012), Independent Parliamentary Inquiry into Online Child Protection: Findings and Recommendations. <https://www.basw.co.uk/resources/independent-parliamentary-inquiry-online-child-protection>

12. Lim MSC, Agius PA, Carrotte ER, Vella AM and Hellard ME (2017). Young Australians' Use of Pornography and Associations with Sexual Risk Behaviours. Aust NZ Journal Public Health Online <https://www.burnet.edu.au/system/asset/file/2649/Pornography_ANZJPH_paper.pdf>

13. Tankard Reist M (2017). Love, sex and no regrets for teens: MTR endorses new book. Melinda Tankard Reist May 18. <http://melindatankardreist.com/2017/06/love-sex-and-no-regrets-for-teens-mtr-endorses-new-book/>

14. Plan Australia (2016). Don't Send Me That Pic: Australian Young Women and Girls Report Online Abuse and Harrassment are Endemic. <https://www.plan.org.au/learn/who-we-are/blog/2016/03/02/dont-send-me-that-pic>

15. Runacres S, Hayes J, Grover S and Temple-Smith M (2015). Exposing the hidden truth about the need for adolescent labiaplasty. Jnl Pediatric Adolescent Gynecology 28(2):e60.

16. https://resistporn.org/parents/. See also Culture Reframed parenting program online.

17. https://resistporn.org/parents/

18. https://resistporn.org/parents/

19. For example, No Fap (for older boys) https://www.nofap.com/; Fight the New Drug (older ages), https://fightthenewdrug.org/, Resistporn.org (faith-based)

20. http://melindatankardreist.com/products-page/

21. www.collectiveshout.com

Understanding self-harm and the difference parents can make

Michelle Mitchell

Michelle is an educator, author and award-winning speaker. In 2000 Michelle left her teaching career and founded Youth Excel, a charity which supported thousands of young people and their families with life skills education, mentoring and psychological services. Today her hands-on experience has made her a sought-after speaker. She presents on topics of well-being, teenage culture and connection. Her work is regularly featured in the media. Michelle has authored *The Excel Series, What Teenage Girls Don't Tell their Parents, Parenting Teenage Girls in the Age of a New Normal* and is soon to release a book on self-harm. She lives in Brisbane with her husband and two teenagers.

www.michellemitchell.org

Michelle Mitchell-author, speaker, educator

@michellemitchellspeaker

Understanding self-harm and the difference parents can make

Twenty years ago, I left my teaching position and founded Youth Excel, a charity which delivered life skills education, mentoring and psychological services to thousands of young people and their families. Looking back over my journey, I can honestly say that some of my most memorable 'career moments' have been with young people who have overcome the desire to self-harm.

Eunice, who I had the privilege of mentoring during her high school years, now accompanies me to some of my presentations to parents and professionals about self-harm. Today she studies psychology at university, but I remember the days when her mother literally mopped pools of blood from the bathroom floor and confiscated razors that seemed to be breeding in her room. Those were days that no mother would want to repeat.

I have seen the absolute helplessness in parents' eyes when they are faced with the brutal reality that they can't control their children's feelings or behaviour. There is nothing more agonising for parents than to see cuts on their daughter's thighs, or bruises or burns on their son's arms, knowing that the behaviour was deliberate and likely to be repeated.

The official term for self-harm is non-suicidal self-injury (NSSI), which simply means deliberately injuring oneself without suicidal intent or ideation.[1] Most young people deliberately injure themselves in an attempt to cope with, express or control emotional pain.[2,3,4] Some use self-harm as a form of self-punishment.[2] Although self-harm may bring temporary relief it is important to note that it does not solve problems.

The 2015 Mental Health Child and Adolescent Report tells us that approximately 10% of young people consciously experiment with self-harm at some stage through high school.[5] Other research estimates self-harm ranges between 7 – 24%, with initiation in the middle school years.[6]

Self-harm is one of those topics which remains very difficult for many adults to understand. "Why would anyone want to hurt themselves?" is the question on most adult's minds. "Why would MY child want to hurt themselves?" is the question that parents whose children are self-harming wrestle with on a daily basis. It seems to go against every innate instinct of self-protection and survival and is therefore a confusing and distressful concept for parents, grandparents, siblings and friends to come to terms with.

The Link to Suicide

When parents find out that their son or daughter is self-harming they often question whether their young person wants to die. However, self-harm can be performed with the intention to die (attempted suicide) or without the intention to die. Rates for non-suicidal self-harm are up to three times higher than self-harm with suicidal intent.[1] Although the link between suicide and self-harm definitely needs to be researched further, there is enough evidence to suggest that self-harm can stand completely independent of suicidal thoughts or actions.

If you are ever concerned about a young person's suicidal tendencies, visit a doctor, hospital or call an ambulance immediately. It is too easy to become familiar with our own children and draw inaccurate conclusions, so an objective opinion is important. A doctor will conduct a suicide risk assessment and provide you with a management plan and referrals to specialists. This management plan may include common sense precautions including removing sharp objects, prescription medication and other high-risk household items. If necessary, they may admit a young person to hospital.

What is clear and consistent through all research is that self-harm is most often linked to poor mental health.[5,7,8,9] Anxiety, depression, and impulsivity are key contributing factors.[3] It takes an open mind for parents to look past self-harm behaviour and towards their young person's general well-being, especially if a young person's mental health has seemed stable in the past.

Types of Self-Harm

The ways in which young people self-harm are wide and varied. Simply google 'creative ways to self-harm' and you will find out how wide and varied they actually are. Some of the less recognised methods include electrocution, burning, self-battery, jumping from dangerous

"...self-harm can stand completely independent of suicidal thoughts or actions."

heights, ceasing medication suddenly, pulling hair, needle sticking, freezing, strangling, suffocating, over-dosing, swallowing a non-ingestible object, train surfing, driving at high speeds and deliberate unsafe sex.

I have seen both males and females hold their breath until they pass out, smash fingertips with a hammer or in a car door, scratch wounds so they won't heal, insert lead from pencils under their skin, burn their skin with lighters or hot water, swallow poisonous substances, jump from heights that they know aren't safe and deliberately bash their limbs against walls so that they break bones.

I would also like to point out that it is the intention of the behaviour which classifies self-harm, rather than the behaviour itself. For example, young people who binge drink may do so for a lot of reasons. They may do so to have fun, gain social status or self-harm, or a combination.

Research from *The Place of Self-Harm in Adolescent Development* puts self-harm into the following categoriess[10]: Cutting (55.9%), Overdosing (22%), Self-battery (11%) and other multiple methods (10%). This explains why self-harm is often called 'cutting'. The multiple methods category is a miscellaneous category which groups together any other form of self-harm which is not defined as cutting, overdosing or self-battery.

Research certainly suggests differences between male and female self-harming tendencies, with males leaning towards high risk behaviour and girls tending towards self-injury.[6] Females were more likely to report self-cutting and overdosing but were less likely to use method such as self-battery or jumping.[8]

"It is so easy for parents of both boys and girls to miss the warning signs of self-harm."

It is so easy for parents of both boys and girls to miss the warning signs of self-harm. One father I interviewed explained, "I noticed cuts on her leg and she told me she had fallen over on sharp grass during PE. I actually believed her at the time. I didn't think about it anymore until I saw cuts on her arm. That is when it clicked. That was at least 2 years ago now. Looking back, I wish I had of been more aware and addressed things earlier."

Some of the common warning signs of self-harm include:

- knowledge of others who are self-harming
- unexplained marks on body
- wearing long sleeves that are never removed
- covering up or wearing baggy clothing
- wearing wide wrist bands that are never removed
- secretive behaviour
- items that could be used for cutting going missing or put in strange places (like the back of drawers)
- needing to be alone for long periods of time
- isolation
- blood stains
- sharp objects found amongst possessions
- frequent stories of accidents
- sleeping and eating changes
- losing interest in usual pleasures
- mood changes

- avoiding situations where arms and legs are showing eg. Gymnastics or swimming carnival
- washing their own clothes
- drop in grades at school

Understanding Self-Harm

Findings from *The Child and Adolescent Self-Harm in Europe CASE Study*[4], helped me a great deal when I ran Youth Excel's Psychology Clinic and was frequently mentoring young people who were self-harming. Being able to hear and recognise young people's specific 'cries', gave me a huge head start in connecting with young people who came to my office. Once I discovered this, I was well on my way to validating their needs and supporting them.

> *"Parents need to think of self-harm as non-verbal language to express either a 'cry of pain' or a 'cry for help'."*

Parents need to think of self-harm as non-verbal language to express either a 'cry of pain' or a 'cry for help'. Both cries are valid requests for specific support. Support can be tailor made once parents understand the underlying motive for self-harm.

A 'cry of pain' motive might sound like a young person who wants to[4],

- get relief from a terrible state of mind
- escape an impossible situation
- punish themselves
- die

A 'cry for help' motive might sound like a young person who wants to[4],

- show how desperate they are feeling
- frighten someone
- get their own back on someone
- find out if someone really loves them
- get someone's attention

Motives for Self-Harm

This common scenario further explains the psychology of self-harm and how a 'cry of pain' or a 'cry for help' interacts with the self-harm process.

Emma wakes up with heightened emotions. She has many assignments due and hasn't slept well. She goes to school and has a fight with a friend who she regularly fights with. She feels alone. Isolated.

When Emma arrives home her mind is racing. She tries to watch TV to distract herself, however she can't stop thinking about that friendship and how things always spiral downhill. She blames herself. She turns to social media (good old social media!) where she notices her friend inviting another girl out on the weekend. The feeling of being alone, staying alone and being picked on intensifies. Maybe all her friends feel the same way about her?!

She has a shower and listens to music. A warm shower usually calms her down, but this time it doesn't. She starts to cry. She hopes to talk to her mum about her day, but her mum is busy. Her mum has just come in from work with a great deal on her mind. Her mum says, "You know what Kirsty is like. Just ignore her and get on with your life. Go and do your homework."

Over the next 40 minutes things go from bad to worse as Emma cycles between crying, looking at her phone, listening to sad music and back again. She tries to settle herself, but nothing seems to be working (or at least quickly enough).

She starts thinking, "I can't cope anymore. If this doesn't stop soon I'm going to do something stupid." For her there is a 'cry of pain' that begins to drive her behaviours. For other young people, there may be a 'cry for help' that says, "If I cut, maybe mum will see how desperate I feel", or "If I cut, Kirsty will see how much this is affecting me."

Young people tell me that they have heard that self-harm works. In Emma's case, Kirsty self-harms and has told Emma that it has been a life saver for her.

Emma takes a blade from her pencil sharpener to cut her thighs. Her body releases endorphins, pain inhibitors. You can liken it to the endorphins which are released after the pain of a good workout or mountain climb. Emma describes an initial high or a rush as these endorphins are released. This signals a change in the chemical state of her body.

Psychologically, a young person's focus turns to the physical pain, the imagery of the blood and the injury. Emma finds that the friendship problems now melt away into the background as secondary issues. The physical pain is a distraction to the emotional pain.

After the rush, Emma then reports a low, or a numbing pain that leads to a shutdown, exhaustion, and crash that throws her body into a recovery period. The knock-on effect of this low is just as addictive as the high. As her body heals, Emma struggles with the guilt and shame associated with her desire to hurt herself. She tries to hide her scars.

Like all destructive behaviour, self-harm is highly addictive because it wires the neurocircuitry of the brain to reach towards self-harm for relief. The more times young people cut, the stronger the 'stress + cutting = relief' circuit becomes.[9]

The Role of the Internet

More than half of young people who report self-harm have previously engaged in internet related searches for self-harm or suicide related material.[11] Similarly, a community study by O-Connor reported that 18% of secondary students were encouraged to self-harm by social networking sites.[11]

There is no doubt that the internet can provide benefits including help seeking, stress alleviation, coping strategies and forums reinforcing positive relationships. However, internet interactions have an overwhelmingly negative impact on participants: normalising self-harm, revealing self-harm techniques and encouraging concealment.[11] It often amplifies the severity of the methods, techniques and frequency of self-harm.[11]

"It is critical that we educate ourselves as parents and have a strong plan for our kids' digital journey from the beginning."

The internet is entwined in almost every issue that families face, self-harm being no exception. We can't deny it's power and influence in our homes. That is why I strongly urge parents of pre-teens to set up gaming and social media in a manner which can withstand the rockiest of the teenage years. It is critical that we educate ourselves as parents and have a strong plan for our kids' digital journey from the beginning.

Developing Resilience

Typically, treatment of self-harm can be challenging.[12] That is why we need to keep our minds open to a variety of intervention methods available to young people. One size does not fit all.

This is my simple, but helpful formula, which I have used time and time again with young people who are in the very early phases of self-harm. This is a great starting place for a young person who is ready to beat self-harm.

As you view these stages, realise that young people may jump between them as they progress. Stages can overlap. Sometimes it may seem like they make progress, only to start back at Stage 1 again. I have found in these cases that progress usually happens quicker and with less support than previously needed.

Stage 1: Professional and Parental Support

When a young person comes to my office for support, their life usually looks like this. They are flapping in the air, out of control with the negatives dominating their life. They usually need the help of a caring adult to lift some of the 'heaviest boxes' out of the way. You will always see the 'big four' when you read about poor mental health – medication, therapy, exercise and sleep. These are usually the big boxes that need moving.

Medication might come in the form of prescription drugs, diet changes or natural remedies. Therapy might include talking to a psychologist, mentor or dedicated family member. Exercise might be as simple as enrolling in a team sport or using a personal trainer. Sleep is a difficult one to control but is usually a by-product of establishing healthy and happy day-to-day routine.

Apps like 'Sleep Cycle' can be used to monitor sleep patterns. Be as creative as necessary in order to move these big boxes out of the way. Be careful to listen to the young person so you hear what is actually working or not working for them.

Stage 2: Self-Care

One of the questions parents ask me the most is, *"When do I step in and when do I let go?"* It can be understandably difficult for parents to let go of a child who has been struggling as they don't want them to encounter any further pain. Once a young person is balancing in the 'middle' position they are reasonably stable. They are out of the danger zone. Things could go up or down at any stage, but they are in a position where they are clear headed enough to make decisions and learn from mistakes.

This is the point where parents need to let go (just enough) for their young person to discover which self-care strategies work for them. These are critical skills that they can't learn if they are over-parented. Therapeutic relationships that help young people develop self-awareness, talk through heavy emotions and implement self-care strategies are usually a critical part of this phase.

Stage 3: Self-Mastery

This is what life looks like when a young person's resources for coping are stronger than their pain. Of course, they don't stay grounded all of the time. Wouldn't that be nice?! However, they have found self-care strategies that work for them and they have the maturity to implement them consistently. We can't expect young people to find this self-mastery overnight. The reality is that this position takes time and practice to master.

Teaching Self-Care

The opposite of self-harm is self-care. Ideally, we want young people to practice self-care to regulate their emotions and avoid the overwhelming spiral that leads to self-harm. Simple in theory, not so simple in practice.

As a foundation for self-care, young people need to develop an awareness of how they feel and recognise when they need to implement self-care strategies. Identifying emotions can be difficult for some young people, especially if they have experienced trauma. In these cases, a psychologist may be the best person to help them identify and express appropriate emotions.

"Ideally, we want young people to practice self-care..."

Emotions demand movement. When emotions are escalating, they quickly move young people in either a positive or negative direction. The good news is that young people can choose which direction they take.

Self-care will always move a young person in a positive direction. Even a negative situation has the capacity to move a young person positively if they understand how to care for themselves. The more educated young people are, the more self-care options they have to choose from.

Emotions, just like waves, have a limited life span. When a young person practices self-care they ride the wave of intense emotion until is passes. It is important to remember that all emotions we experience, whether happy or sad, have a limited life span. Self-care is a courageous decision to make, because it takes effort and strength.

The basic premise for riding an emotional wave can be seen in Carol Vivyan's 3D's journal activity which I saw on the wall of a school classroom many years ago.[13]

> *"...all emotions we experience, whether happy or sad, have a limited life span."*

Delay
Delay giving into the urge of self-harm for a set amount of time. You get to decide on how long that time will be. You can set a timer if you want to ensure you stick to the time you decide on.

Distract
Participate in an activity that can occupy your thoughts and channel your energy in a positive direction. Write a list of things you could do. This list can be written in advance.

Decide
After the set period, decide how you are going to respond to the urge. Write down the advantages and disadvantages of delaying the urge again, if it is still there.

Young people may consider a wider range of self-care strategies that may help them ride a wave of intense emotions. Each individual will have a preference or type of self-care which works best for them, based on why they self-harm, and the typical length of time between their thoughts about self-harming and corresponding actions.

Apps that I recommend and work with

- #selfcare
- Calm Harm
- Mood Path

- The Breathing APP
- Sleep Cycle
- Smiling Mind
- The Resilience Project
- Headspace

The 'Calm Harm' app guides young people through a similar process to the 3D Journal Activity.

Self-Care Strategies

Knowing how to manage emotions and comfort yourself when you are unhappy or distressed is a skill that can take anyone a long time to learn. Even grown adults look for someone else to comfort and rescue them! Why? Because it takes self-perception to find strategies that truly work especially because we are always growing and evolving as human beings.

There are a wide range of strategies that young people can use to self-care. Each individual will have a preference or type of self-care which works best for them, based on why they self-harm, and the typical length of time between their thoughts about self-harming and corresponding actions. I'd like to finish this article with a list of self-care strategies that young people might use to ride out waves of intense emotions.

Creative self-care strategies include:
- story writing
- painting, drawing and other art forms
- journaling
- composing music or playing instruments
- compiling music playlists
- putting on makeup or styling hair
- learning a new skill or art form

Soothing self-care strategies include:
- taking a warm bath or shower
- putting on comfortable clothes
- buying different textured socks

- drinking hot milk
- cuddling a teddy bear or blanket
- getting a massage
- putting on perfume or lighting a scented candle
- watching TV or a movie
- meditation

Organising self-care strategies include:
- sorting a wardrobe
- cleaning a bedroom
- building something
- reorganising makeup
- finishing homework or assignments

Social self-care strategies include:
- phoning a friend
- being with a friend
- helping someone else in need
- going to a public place
- gaming with friends
- watching funny you tube videos with friends
- playing with a pet

Physical self-care strategies include:
- riding a bike or going for a run
- dancing
- squeezing something
- making a loud noise
- ripping something
- punching something
- eating something with a strong taste

Strategies I Have Seen Work

One strategy I have seen work is asking young people to draw the name of someone they love in the place that they usually self-harm. Alternatively, they could put a fake tattoo or an inspiring quote in that place. This may act as a reminder as to why they are choosing not to self-harm. Sometimes young people will do something for someone else that they won't do for themselves.

Another strategy that I have seen work is replacing self-harm with body painting. I encourage parents to buy soft paintbrushes of varying sizes and colourful paints so young people can paint their arms, legs or other parts of their body that they would usually harm. Young people tell me that the 'sensory experience is soothing, and the strokes of colour bring hope'. One chaplain contacted me and explained how she uses body paint in her role, "I now have a few pots of body paint in my chappy room, and some coloured eyeliner pencils for 'henna tattoo' art that young people can use if they are feeling overwhelmed. It's a great alternative to self-harming."

Final Thoughts

If you have a child who is struggling with self-harm, I want to remind you that YOU are your child's greatest advantage. The psychologist you are paying will add value, but they can't replace you. The chaplain at the school that you have invested so much hope into will add value, but they can't replace you either. You are uniquely graced to parent your children and you are irreplaceable in their lives. You are their constant. Your connection with them is everything in their self-discovery and recovery.

I often say that parenting is usually difficult when you are doing a good job of it. This is especially true when parenting a young person who is struggling with self-harm. There is no doubt that self-harm will test every ounce of patience, strength and love that a parent can muster. There is also no doubt that a loving parent somehow finds all these attributes and more when they are required of them.

Parents often feel isolated when they first discover self-harm and are unsure where to turn. Although self-harm is a confronting topic, it is one which I feel is incredibly important to shed light on. I believe that through more honest and open discussion we can more effectively help young people stay calm cope well and live their best lives.

For More Information

Michelle's book, *SELF-HARM: Why Teens Do It and What Parents Can Do To Help* provides more comprehensive discussion on self-harm and the new phenomenon digital self-harm.

Footnotes

1. J. Kidger, J. Heron, G. Lewis, J. Evans and D. Gunnell, "Adolesecent self-harm and suicidal thoughts in teh ALSPAC cohort: a self-report survey in England," *BMC Psychiatry*, 2012.

2. D. Klonsky, "The funtions of self-injury in young adults who cut themselves: claritying the evidence for affect regulation," *Psychiatry Res*, vol. 166, pp. 260 - 268, 2010.

3. N. Madge, K. Hawton, E. Mchan, P. Carcoran, D. D. Leo, E. J. d. Wilde, S. Fekete, K. v. Heeringen, M. Ystgaard and E. Arensman, "Psychological Characteristics, stressful life events and deliberate self-harm: Findings from the Child and Adolescent Self-Harm in Europe (CASE) Study," *Eur Child Psychiatry*, p. 498, 2011.

4. G. Scoliers, G. Portzyky, N. Madge, A. Hewitt, K. Hawton, E. J. d. Wilde, M. Ystgaard, E. Arensman, D. D. Leo, S. Fekete and K. v. Heeringen, "Reasons for Adolescent Deliberate Self-Harm: A Cry of Pain and/or a Cry for Help?," *Soc Psychiatry Psychiatr Epidemiol*, p. 601, 2008.

5. D. Lawrence, S. Johnson, J. Hafekost, K. B. d. Hann, J. A. Michael Sawyer and S. R. Zubrick, The Mental Health of Children and Adolescents Survey of Mental Health and Wellbeing, Paper-based publications, 2015.

6. M. A. Moreno, A. Ton, E. Selkie and Y. Evans, "Secret Society 123: Understanding the Language of Self-Harm on Instagram," *Journal of Adolscent Health*, p. 78, 2015.

7. K. Hawton, K. Sunders and R. O'Connor, "Self-harm and suicide in adolescents," *The Lancet*, vol. 379, pp. 2373 - 2382, 2012.

8. N. Madge, a. Hewitt, K. Hawton, E. J. d. Wilde, P. Corcoran, S. Fekete, K. c. Heeringen, D. D. Leo and M. Ystgaard, "Deliberate Self-harm with an international community sample of young people: comparative findings from the child and adolescent self-harm in Europe (CASE) study," *The Journal of Child Psychology and Psychiatry*, p. 667, 2008.

9. R. T.Liu, "Characterising the course of non-suicidal self-injury: A cognitive neuroscience perspecitve," *Neuroscience and Biobehavioral Reviews*, p. 159, 2017.

10. R. J. R. Levesque, "Special Issue Introduction: The Place of Self-Harm in Adolescent Development," *J Youth Adolescence*, p. 217, 2009.

11. N. Jacob, R. Evans and J. Scourfield, "The Influence of online images on self-harm: A qualitative study of young people aged 16 - 24," *Journal of Adolescence*, p. 140, 2017.

12. D. Klonsky, "The function of self-injury in young adults who cut themselves," *Psychiatry Res*, pp. 260 - 268, 2010.

13. C. Vivyan, "www.get.gg," 2011. [Online]. Available: https://www.getselfhelp.co.uk.

Collett Smart

Collett Smart is a psychologist, qualified teacher and author.

Collett has more than 20 years' experience working in private and public schools, as well as in private practice. She appears regularly on national television and radio, as an expert in teen and family issues. Collett has taught and delivered psychology workshops and seminars around the world. She is an Ambassador for International Justice Mission Australia and is mum to 3 children.

She has recently published her first book, *They'll Be Okay: 15 Conversations To Help Your Child Through Troubled Times.*

www.collettsmart.com

Collett Smart – psychologist

@collettsmart

@collettsmart

The Power
of Gratitude

"In ordinary life we hardly realise that we receive a great deal more than we give, and that it is only with gratitude that life becomes rich."

Dietrich Bonhoeffer – German theologian and anti-Nazi dissident (1906-1945)

One of the key factors for developing resilience in children (among those already mentioned in this book) is cultivating a positive outlook in life. A positive outlook involves both optimism and gratitude, and this is something we all recognise as important for our kids' healthy development.

Most of us would easily recognise an adult who has not developed a habit of gratitude. They are the person who routinely complains and demands things from others, and just never seem content. They can be quite unpleasant to be around. Really, what we are witnessing is entitlement – the opposite of gratitude. People don't arrive at entitlement overnight. Which means, as parents and educators, if we invest time into consciously teaching our children to develop a habit of looking for the good, looking for moments and people to be thankful for, we can build resilience and inoculate our kids against entitlement.

Every culture recognises the importance of saying thank you. Many Western parents would have begun with teaching the foundations of gratitude the day we handed a baby rusk to our tot and uttered the word, 'Ta!' In several cultures people use their whole bodies to express gratitude. For example, some cultures deem it more sincere to accept a gift using both hands, or to clap their hands together and then open their palms before receiving something. Others demonstrate thanks by pressing both palms together in front of the chest, and the Japanese custom is to bow as one display of gratitude.

It is important however, to recognise that an attitude of gratitude is more than a gesture or saying the words, "Thank you". One study found that eighty-five percent of parents, encouraged their children to say thank you and show gratitude in ways consistent with good manners, but only half said that their children demonstrated gratitude in ways that went beyond gestures of 'good manners'. In other words, although remembering to say 'Thanks', as the canteen lady hands your child their lunch, is a wonderful display of basic manners, this does not necessarily mean your child has developed a grateful mind-set. These findings suggest that there are more opportunities for fostering gratitude in our children, that are yet to be tapped.

"An attitude of gratitude is more than a gesture or saying the words, 'Thank you'."

Gratitude isn't a mind-set that develops overnight, especially if your child has a habit of leaning towards bitterness, anger or negative thinking, but it's something everyone can learn with practice. If we think of gratitude like a muscle, which needs a regular workout to become strong and healthy, this helps us to be patient with our children as they grow in this area. Consider your home to be like a gratitude gym, where you are the kind and gracious coach, preparing your children for the arena of life. Particularly because resilience is often developed in times when things are tough, and when we don't immediately see something to be grateful for. Our kids will need our compassionate guidance in these times.

Kids need support and opportunities to practice gratitude, but above all they need a parent's example. So even though gratitude can be a difficult new habit for some kids to form, once it begins to develop it is incredibly powerful!

Defining gratitude

Robert Emmons[1], a leading expert on gratitude, believes that gratitude has two key components. I will call these 'affirmation' and 'the other'.

1. **It begins with 'affirmation'**

    Gratitude begins with an affirmation of goodness. In this component Emmons says we acknowledge that there are good things in the world; gifts and benefits we've received. Importantly, this does not ignore pain and it does not mean life is perfect. Rather, when we look at life as a whole, he believes that gratitude encourages us to identify some amount of goodness in our lives.

2. **Gratitude recognises 'the other'**

    The second part of gratitude is in teaching children to figure out where that goodness comes from. Emmon believes, it is important to help kids to recognise the sources of this goodness as being outside of themselves. He calls gratitude a 'social emotion', because it requires us to notice how we've been supported and affirmed by others. i.e children, learn to consider the sacrifice and kindness that other people have shown them.

Naturally we can (and should) encourage children to appreciate positive traits or skills in themselves. When they recognise they have worked hard at something, reached out to others or achieved goals they set, children develop a sense of self-worth. However, gratitude involves a recognition of a humble dependence on others, even as we grow our own skills. Many sport, art or academic achievers reached their potential because of the dedication, sacrifice and kindness of parents or coaches. Dads who drove them to weekly training, waited in the rain and cheered them on at events. Mums who gave up their weekends or evenings to coach teams, because they believed in the team's potential – even when they didn't reach a PB (Personal Best).

Learning to communicate gratitude teaches children that life is about more than individual desires. That parents, siblings or friends are not there to simply serve their needs. Gratitude recognises others and communicates an appreciation of others. It gives children opportunities to practice using a complex set of socio-emotional skills. i.e using language as a means of expression, communicating and relating to others in healthy ways, perceiving what others might need and how you might behave or respond in that moment. It also provides opportunities for developing **empathy** – trying to understand or imagine yourself in another person's place, rather than from your own point of view.

Consequently, when we thank our children for their help and support in our lives, or recognise a selfless act, we model to them what these socio-emotional skills look and feel like.

What gratitude is not

Gratitude does not mean we teach our children to be pushovers. Resilient Kids learn that we don't expect them to display gratitude just because someone is in a place of authority. And most certainly never when something is abusive. Resilient Kids are assertive and can stand up for themselves. However, they know how to look outward and consider others, and they don't lash out when things don't always go their way. Abuse aside, Resilient Kids learn to look for the good in each situation.

"Resilient Kids are assertive and can stand up for themselves."

Gratitude is also not a *feeling* – gratitude is a *choice*.[2] We need to help our children to understand that they don't need to wait to feel something before they express gratitude. This is where the power of gratitude lies. Choosing to act with gratitude, even when we don't immediately *feel* grateful, is shown to have positive effects on people struggling with depression or anxiety.[3] Cultivating gratitude in our homes means we help children to choose to hold a positive prevailing attitude about life. Of course this perspective is not easy at the start – but as I mentioned – it gets better with practice.

What the research tells us about the benefits gratitude

Overall gratitude is good for all of us physically, psychologically and socially.[4]

Physically – We sleep better, have better energy levels and improved heart health.[5] Gratitude profoundly affects the body. Thankful people have lower blood pressure, stronger immunity, and a higher tendency to stick to eating in healthy ways and maintain good exercise habits.[6]

Psychologically – Gratitude is associated with improved self-esteem, greater happiness and resilience.[7] Gratitude allows people to celebrate the present. Their minds are more focussed on what they already have, rather than what they don't have. It has been shown that practising thankfulness actually changes the structure of the brain and pulls the brain out of negative-thinking ruts. In particular, taking the time to record just three things that one is grateful for each day, over just a 2-week period, is shown to reduce stress and increase well-being.[8]

> *"Practising thankfulness actually changes the structure of the brain and pulls the brain out of negative-thinking ruts.*

Socially – I believe we are made for relationships and so we are happier because gratitude is such a social emotion. It cultivates in us a sense that we are connected to others. It's in these connections with friends, family and neighbours that we find the true stuff of happiness. When we choose gratitude it improves empathy toward others, driving us to be more helpful, compassionate and forgiving.

In young people specifically, evidence[9,10] suggests that gratitude leads them to be happier, more optimistic, less envious, depressed and materialistic. They have better social support, are more satisfied with their school, family, community, friends, and themselves. They also give more emotional support to others and use their strengths to better their community.

What incredible benefits!

What can we do to cultivate gratitude in our homes?

We've learned that gratitude is a skill. You aren't simply born with or without it. This is good news, because it is something that can be taught to our children. Although, each child is different and researchers agree that not every gratitude strategy works for every child.

I keep saying this, but we must begin by modelling gratitude in our homes. As with anything, our children won't learn gratitude just because we say they should, while we continue to behave in opposite ways. Secondly, we need to be deliberate in our approach and find opportunities to notice and talk about gratitude in our daily family lives.[11]

Based on the scientific literature and their conversations with parents, the Raising Grateful Children project came to think about teaching gratitude as something that has four components:[12]

- What we **NOTICE** in our lives for which we can be grateful

- How we **THINK** about why we have been given those things

- How we **FEEL** about the things we have been given

- What we **DO** to express appreciation in turn

Using the Raising Grateful Children project framework as a model, here are some of my suggestions for how we might put these into practice and cultivate gratitude in our everyday family lives:

NOTICE

- **Notice out loud** when your child displays gratitude. This helps them develop self-awareness. Talk about gratitude – often, and tell your children when you have noticed them being helpful at home or demonstrated kindness to a sibling, pet or friend. You might say, "Thank you so much for doing the dishwasher yesterday, it really helped me by not having to cook among the clutter." or, "Thank you for being such a wonderful big sister. I noticed how kindly you spoke to your brother when he was upset yesterday."

- **Start small** – You might use family meal times, which are shown to have enormous benefits[13], to communicate that gratitude is an important part of your family values. For example, in our home we ask each person at the table to, "Tell us about one not very good thing that happened in your day, and then list one good thing/something you are grateful for today."

- **Bedtime rituals** – Incorporate teaching children to have a thankful heart as part of their bedtime ritual. E.g. Ask, "Can you tell me about one activity, action or person you are grateful for today, and then I will tell you mine?"

Alternatively, ask your child to consider, "What do you think you already have in your life, which you are grateful for?" (these need to extend beyond material items). Follow this by asking your child to give a brief reason why. Asking why they chose these examples helps them think a little more deeply about where the goodness came from, and how others might have made a sacrifice or showed kindness.

- **Ask open ended questions** about positive life events (holidays, parties etc). This helps children to notice their thoughts and feelings at the time, and encourages them to recall things they can be grateful for. E.g "Tell me about the gifts, behind the material gifts you received today, which you are grateful for?"

- **When gratitude is absent** – Notice and talk about times when gratitude is not there. I.e missed opportunities to be grateful. This must be done gently and kindly – not in a way that might embarrass or shame your child. Wonder with your child what got in the way of gratitude. Was it excitement, entitlement, distraction, embarrassment? These will provide insight into your child's development and mind-set and can help them think about gratitude differently in the next situation.

THINK

- **Gifts and skills** – Help your children to think about the gifts and skills they have. i.e. "Why do you think you received that gift or skill?"

- **Others' involvement** – Encourage children to think about how others have helped them to develop or pursue their skills. E.g. "Do you think the help or support was something the giver/coach/friend had to give you?"

- **Recognising others' support** – Help children recognise and consider others' kindness or self-sacrifice in their lives. E.g. "Do you think you owe the giver something in return?" or "Do you think you earned the gift because of something you did on your own?"

"Encourage children to think about how others have helped them to develop or pursue their skills."

- **When things are tough** – Opportunities to think about gratitude in times of failure, pain or hardship are essential to character building and the development of resilience. Naturally, this is never easy and we should wait until the intensity of the moment has passed, before encouraging reflection on gratitude. At the right time, we might ask, "What you went through last week seemed to be very painful. Is there anyone you noticed that was particularly kind or supportive of you in that time?"

FEEL

- **Connecting emotions** – To understand gratitude, children need opportunities to connect positive feelings with certain gifts, or with another's display of kindness, help or sacrifice. "What does it feel like inside, to receive this gift/ get help with your batting practice today?" or "What is it about this gift that made you feel happy/loved/cared about?"

- **Modelling emotional expression** – Model to your children how you feel when something is done for you. Perhaps send appreciation texts to family members telling them how their action or gift made you feel.

- **Unconditional regard** – Tell your children how grateful you feel about them simply being in your life. You might say something like, "I feel like the luckiest mum in the world, that you are my son." Or "I am so thankful that you are just the way you are."

- **Affirmation or appreciation notes** – Put notes into young children's lunchboxes or under your teen's pillow, as concrete displays of gratitude and affirmation.
  E.g. "I felt so proud of you when you told me how you stood by your friend yesterday. I am sure she is so grateful to have such a loyal friend."

- **During hard times** you might ask, "You expressed great disappointment that your team lost the finals last week. Is there anyone on the team you might have been thankful for during the season?" or "Is there anything that you could be grateful for in that situation, because it taught you something new about yourself/your friend/the situation?"

"I am so thankful that you are just the way you are."

DO

- **Encourage** children to say 'thank you' to others in their lives: friends, teachers, coaches, Grandma, etc. You might first ask, "Is there a way you want to show someone how you feel about this gift?" Perhaps this might be in the form of 'thank you' letters or texts. Help them to be specific in their thanks – and not just for the big things, but the everyday stuff they do.

> *"Encourage children to say 'thank you' to others in their lives."*

- **Journals** – Buy each child a personal gratitude journal (or box) where they can reflect on the good things they have in their lives. This can be particularly helpful for children and teens struggling with metal health issues.

- **The 'Grateful For You Jar'** – This is a family jar where each one pops in a note to every family member once a week. These can be read out once a month or in times when siblings are going through a period of conflict. This might include gratitude for acts of kindness, selfless acts or personality traits you appreciate, and how these made each person feel.

- **The Gratitude board** – Instead of the jar you might use a family gratitude whiteboard, where 2 points of combined family gratitude can be added each day over a few weeks. (Only do this for short periods of time, a few times a year before children become bored with it and it loses its value.)

- **Pay it forward** – Finally, we need to take steps to consider how the gifts, sacrifices and kindness of others could prompt us, and our children, to 'pay it forward'. Connecting the abundance that we have with a sense that it isn't just ours to horde is a healthy value to model to children. That our gifts and skills are something we can develop into a form of active gratitude i.e "How might we contribute to others, give back to our community/to the world?"

Active gratitude

When we volunteer, there is a subtle shift that happens within ourselves. As human beings, when we work for something greater than ourselves, we develop moral character. When giving and volunteering become a family habit, we actively teach children about the value of others, especially those who are vulnerable.

Helping others evokes feelings of gratitude, compassion, and confidence in people, including young children.[14] We now know that volunteering is good for both the mind[15] and the body[16] across cultures[17], because it diminishes loneliness and social isolation through building community and developing a solid support system. It also enhances social skills, builds mental strength, increases self-confidence and life satisfaction. It has even been shown to lessen symptoms of chronic pain or heart disease. But most importantly, volunteering teaches us that everyone is valuable, thus developing ethical behaviour. Children who volunteer are more likely to grow up to be adults with these skills.

Active gratitude ideas need not be onerous for your family. Perhaps pick one or two a year, that strengthen your family values and fit in with your children's ages and routines. Here are some ideas:

- Donate to a food pantry – children can help choose items.

- Create Christmas boxes for charities.

- Walk or run to raise funds to fight a disease.

- Encourage teens to coach younger teams in a sport they love.

- Put together books, toys, games or activity boxes for children at a local hospital.

- Take muffins and treats to the staff on duty at nursing homes, fire or police stations on public holidays.

- Clean up your local park, neighbourhood or beach (supervise your children closely while doing this).

- Deliver meals to an elderly neighbour or someone who is ill.

- Volunteer to help look after a neighbour's pet or do respite care at local animal shelters.

- Support and become involved with advocacy groups, charity groups or sponsor child organisations.

Gratitude has the potential to change your child's life. It inoculates them against entitlement and provides them with a perspective from which they will begin to look at life as a whole package, and not become overwhelmed when something goes wrong. This is the basis for Raising Resilient Kids.

Footnotes

1. Emmons, R. A. (2013). Gratitude works!: A 21-day program for creating emotional prosperity. John Wiley & Sons.

2. Griffith, O. M. (2016). *Gratitude: A Way of Teaching*. Rowman & Littlefield.

3. Wong, Y. J., Owen, J., Gabana, N. T., Brown, J. W., McInnis, S., Toth, P., & Gilman, L. (2018). Does gratitude writing improve the mental health of psychotherapy clients? Evidence from a randomized controlled trial. *Psychotherapy Research*, 28(2), 192-202.

4. Elosúa, M. R. (2015). The influence of gratitude in physical, psychological, and spiritual well-being. *Journal of Spirituality in Mental Health*, 17(2), 110-118.

5. Mills, P. J., Redwine, L., Wilson, K., Pung, M. A., Chinh, K., Greenberg, B. H., ... & Chopra, D. (2015). The role of gratitude in spiritual well-being in asymptomatic heart failure patients. *Spirituality in clinical practice*, 2(1), 5.

6. U C Davis Health (2015, November 25). Gratitude is good medicine - Practicing gratitude boosts emotional and physical well-being. Retrieved from https://health.ucdavis.edu/welcome/features/2015-2016/11/20151125_gratitude.html

7. Park, N., & Peterson, C. (2006). Character strengths and happiness among young children: Content analysis of parental descriptions. *Journal of Happiness Studies*, 7(3), 323-341.

8. Krejtz, I., Nezlek, J. B., Michnicka, A., Holas, P., & Rusanowska, M. (2016). Counting one's blessings can reduce the impact of daily stress. *Journal of Happiness Studies*, 17(1), 25-39.

9. Froh, J. J., Bono, G (2014, March 5). Seven Ways to Foster Gratitude in Kids. Retrieved from https://greatergood.berkeley.edu/article/item/seven_ways_to_foster_gratitude_in_kids

10. Bono, G., Froh, J. J., Disabato, D., Blalock, D., McKnight, P., & Bausert, S. (2019). Gratitude's role in adolescent antisocial and prosocial behavior: A 4-year longitudinal investigation. *The Journal of Positive Psychology*, 14(2), 230-243.

11. Hussong, A. M., Langley, H. A., Rothenberg, W. A., Coffman, J. L., Halberstadt, A. G., Costanzo, P. R., & Mokrova, I. (2018). Raising grateful children one day at a time. *Applied Developmental Science*, 1-14.

12. Hussong, A. M. (2017, November 21). What Parents Neglect to Teach about Gratitude. Retrieved from https://greatergood.berkeley.edu/article/item/what_parents_neglect_to_teach_about_gratitude

13. Cook, E., & Dunifon, R. (2012). *Do Family Meals Really Make a Difference?*. Cornell University, College of Human Ecology, http://www. human. cornell. edu/pam/outreach/upload/Family-Mealtimes2. pdf (accessed October, 30, 2018).

14. Aknin, L. B., Hamlin, J. K., & Dunn, E. W. (2012). Giving leads to happiness in young children. *PLoS One*, 7(6), e39211.

15. Corporation for National, Community Service (US). Office of Research, & Policy Development. (2007). *The health benefits of volunteering: A review of recent research*. Corporation for National & Community Service,[Office of Research and Policy Development.

16. Harris, A. H., & Thoresen, C. E. (2005). Volunteering is associated with delayed mortality in older people: analysis of the longitudinal study of aging. *Journal of Health Psychology*, 10(6), 739-752.

17. Kumar, S., Calvo, R., Avendano, M., Sivaramakrishnan, K., & Berkman, L. F. (2012). Social support, volunteering and health around the world: Cross-national evidence from 139 countries. *Social science & medicine*, 74(5), 696-706.

Michael Grose

Michael Grose is one of Australia's leading parenting educators. He's the author of ten books for parents including his latest release, *Spoonfed Generation: How to raise independent kids*.

A trailblazer in the parenting and educational scenes, Michael regularly appears in the media throughout Australia in programs such as *The Today Show*, *Studio 10* and ABC radio.

Michael was recognised for his contribution to parenting and education when he was elevated to the PSA Speaker Hall of Fame in 2013. He is the past winner of the PSA Australian Educator of the Year Award.

Michael was the first person to conduct a parenting seminar to Federal politicians in Parliament House, Canberra. He's also the parent of three children who have successfully flown the nest.

www.parentingideas.com.au

Parenting Ideas

@_parentingIdeas

Helping kids manage anxiety

Carefree, relaxed and enjoying the quintessential happy childhood: this is what we all want for our kids. But for an increasing number of children and teens, their participation in and enjoyment of life is affected by anxiety; an emotion that they don't understand, can't shake and would do anything to be free from. While a normal emotion under stressful circumstances, anxiety becomes a problem when it continues long after the stressor has passed, detracting from their happiness and the quality of their lives.

And it's more prevalent than ever. According to Australian mental health agency beyondblue, one in seven young Australians experience a mental illness and, of those, half have an anxiety disorder. When anxiety is unmanaged and untreated, it gets worse over time, not better. Concurrent research shows that when anxiety goes unmanaged in childhood it will reoccur in adulthood.

The good news is that anxiety is manageable and parents are in the ideal position to assist children and young people to manage anxiousness before it becomes a disorder. First, we need to understand the origins of anxiousness and learn strategies to assist children and young people to better manage anxiety.

What is anxiety?

Anxiety is the body's response to fear, real or perceived. It's our body's way of protecting us when we're in danger. It's completely normal to feel anxious from time to time. A child might feel anxious about speaking in front of their class, or a teen might feel anxious about an exam. Those anxious feelings can act as a motivator to do more revision or be better prepared. With 'normal' anxiety, when the stressful event has passed, the anxious feelings pass too. However many children and young people continue to experience feelings of anxiety when, in fact, there is little or nothing to be feared.

Fellow parenting educator, Dr Jodi Richardson has a wonderful way of describing anxiety. She likens the anxiety response to a smoke alarm. She says, "The alarm is designed to alert us to fire, a danger that can threaten our lives. In a similar way, our anxiety response is a protective system, designed to protect us from life-threatening danger. If our fight or flight system simply got us activated to escape real danger, the way a smoke detector does in a house fire, then there's no problem. But when it stays on way after the danger has passed, then life can become very difficult."

> "Anxiety becomes a problem when it starts interfering with daily life."

Continuing the smoke alarm metaphor, Jodi maintains that anxiety becomes a problem when the mind's alarm system is sensitive and responds when there's no genuine danger present. It's as if the body's alarm system sounds in response to the equivalent of burnt toast. Anxiety becomes a problem when it starts interfering with daily life. Many children and teenagers experience the symptoms of anxiety when they're actually quite safe and the danger is only imagined. And sometimes anxiety shows up for no reason at all.

The fight or flight response is not meant to be activated all the time. It's a combination of reactions to stress or danger, triggered by the part of our brain called the amygdala. It prepares the body in a variety of ways to stand up and fight the danger or flee. It triggers a cascade of hormones that result in physical changes that 'power up' the body for conflict or rapid escape. Sometimes the reaction can be to freeze, where the body and mind feel paralysed. All these changes occur suddenly and involve a range of emotions from unpleasantness, to feeling completely overwhelmed with worry and feelings of futility.

Why children and young people are so anxious

There's no doubt there is genetic connection to anxiety. Simply, some children are born to worry. It's in their nature and most likely it's reinforced by spending time with a parent who also experiences anxiety. Frequently, adults who experience anxiety are unaware of their reactions. People can live with anxiety for decades and only become aware when a significant mental health problem causes them to pause and take stock. As one sixty-something gentleman recently said, "I've been anxious all my life but I didn't know. I thought those horrible feelings were normal." I suspect there are many people reading this who regularly feel anxious about seemingly small events yet they continue to soldier on. Those difficult feelings generally catch up with us eventually, negatively impacting on our quality of life. Living with anxiety is tiring and wears even the strongest person down in the end.

People frequently ask me why so many kids are anxious, when we enjoy such a high standard of living, and live in a country with a stable government. What's going on? Anxiety is very personal and can occur even in the most affluent of conditions. However, it's becoming evident that children are experiencing anxiety at higher levels today than ever. I believe there are four main reasons for this epidemic of anxiety:

Adults pass their anxiety and stresses on to kids

Anxiety is a function of groups – it rarely happens in isolation. Many parents I meet in my work are stressed by their lives and fearful for their children. The contagious nature of anxiety means that parents often pass their stresses, worries and fears on to their children. Founder of the Positive Psychology movement

> *"The contagious nature of anxiety means that parents often pass their stresses, worries and fears on to their children."*

Martin Seligman found through his research that children by the age of eight have a significant propensity to copy their primary parents' explanatory styles. If parents see events through the frame of stress, anxiety and fear then they are passing this same frame on to their children. Yep, we adults as a group are a stressed bunch right now.

Children and teens are overloaded

Few would argue that an active child is a healthy child. However, it seems that we now have too much of a good thing as Australian kids have a smorgasbord of organised pre-school and after-school activities, to keep their minds and bodies active. Many of these activities have a high-performance element attached (get that badge, win that game, attain that level) so that kids are always striving or attaining. The pressure to perform is always there. Activity overload is a particular problem for achievement-driven, anxious types of kids, which are classic first-born child characteristics. And we have more firstborns than ever as a percentage of the population.

Children and teenagers don't play enough

Play is the release valve for the pressures of a high performance, serious life. It's the way kids have always relaxed and let off steam. The best type of play for relaxing and letting off steam is generally physical play that takes place outside. A child may play a great deal on a digital device, but this activity over-stimulates the brain rather than rejuvenates it. Kids need less screen-time and more green time for good mental health.

Organised sport doesn't fit the play category if it adds to their anxiety rather than releases it. Some children and teenagers find organised sport to be stressful rather than relaxing. Kids need to be involved in play that's fun, rejuvenating and enjoyable. They need to look forward to it rather than fear it.

Children and teens can focus too much on the future

Some children are born worriers. They fret about seemingly simple activities such as starting a new school term, going to a birthday party or about who's picking them up from school at the end of the day. Worriers are future oriented, anxious about things that haven't happened yet. These type-A anxious types don't know how to stay in the present. Their minds constantly wander ahead to what may happen. They benefit from learning relaxation techniques, such as mindfulness and deep breathing that anchor them to the present, temporarily releasing them from their worries and anxieties. When kids learn these techniques from a young age, or even during adolescence, they are likely to become hard-wired for life.

Responding in the moment to a child or teenager's anxiety

Parents are well positioned to assist kids to manage their anxiousness by teaching them critical self-regulation skills. It's essential that we model healthy ways of responding to stress and anxiety-inducing situations.

Children and teenagers see their parents at very close quarters. They witness many of our happiest moments and so see us at our best, and they see how we approach stressful and challenging situations as well. They see if we avoid challenges or if we take a big breath and tackle head-on. These are tremendously important lessons for kids to learn. It's the behaviours they witness when adults are under stress that usually have the greatest impact on children. If we blow issues out of all proportion then there is every likelihood that children will think that catastrophising is an acceptable response mechanism to situations that challenge them. When we respond thoughtfully and calmly to a difficult situation, we show our kids how to respond in similar ways. So how should we respond when kids are anxious?

> *"When we respond thoughtfully and calmly to a difficult situation, we show our kids how to respond in similar ways."*

Empathy always

When they're feeling anxious, the very first thing kids need to know is that we understand how they feel. When we show empathy, anxious kids feel validated. Empathy demonstrates that we know what it feels like to experience fear, anxiety and worry.

If we stay too calm then an anxious child may think that we don't understand them. This can lead to them turning up the dial on their emotions and behaviour so we eventually do get it. We don't have to agree with their reaction or what they're saying, but a powerful first response to anxiety is to validate how they're feeling.

Use Ahhh! statements

An Ahhhh! Statement is a practical way to validate how a child is feeling and to remind them that their thoughts are not facts. Repeating back what we're hearing shows we're listening and trying to understand. It's also a great way to help children develop a more nuanced emotional vocabulary. Here are some examples:

"Ahhhh, you're feeling anxious right now…"

"Ahhhh, you're having one of those 'I might mess it up' ideas…"

"Ahhhh, you're feeling disappointed that didn't work out for you…"

Okay, now breathe

When it comes to calming down anxiety, the brain 'listens' to the body. Kids and teens can show their brain that they're safe with deep, slow breathing. This type of breathing helps bring their brain down from high alert and signals the nervous system to begin to return to normal. Encourage kids to practise deep breathing in between times of high anxiety. By practising, they're preparing their body to calm down using breathing when the fight or flight response is in full swing. If a child is anxious, remind them to breathe. "Come on let's take three big belly breaths together."

"Encourage kids to practise deep breathing in between times of high anxiety."

Bring kids back to the present

Generally, kids become anxious about future events, such as giving a talk, starting secondary school or going into an unfamiliar situation. They can be perfectly safe yet their bodies respond as if they are in danger because they are thinking about what may happen. Mindfulness is a great tool to bring kids into the present and relieve them of their feelings of anxiousness. Next time you feel tense, go outside, stand still and call out five things you can see. This simple mindfulness activity is guaranteed to shut down the mental clutter and bring your focus to the present moment.

Try exercise to dissipate anxiety

Exercise plays a huge role in anxiety management, yet children's lifestyles are increasingly sedentary. Exercise and movement helps kids regulate their moods and reduces the symptoms of anxiety. Play and exercise help to ease muscle tension, regulate breathing, induce the release of 'feel-good' neurotransmitters and stimulate the production of the neurotransmitters associated with decreased anxiety and improved mood.

Tune kids into their thoughts

Thought-noticing is a wonderful skillset which helps kids to better manage their mental health. When kids tune into their thinking, they can immediately distance themselves from it. Rather than being lost in the thoughts that are making them feel anxious, they can mentally step back and see the thought for what it is – a thought which comes and goes, and not a fact.

"Thought-noticing is a wonderful skillset which helps kids to better manage their mental health."

Guide them to take action toward what matters

Kids often want to avoid activities and situations that make them anxious. This is natural; however, avoidance simply ensures that the anxiety about the activity or event will reappear next time. Help kids identify what's important and guide them toward doing the things that they want. Gradual exposure to an activity or an event can help when kids are really struggling.

Independence helps lessen anxiety

It would be silly to suggest that an autonomous child would never experience anxiety. However, there is no doubt that greater levels of autonomy lead to decreasing levels of anxiety in children and young people in the long term. Independence builds personal capacities in kids. By doing things for themselves they develop a great level of skills, giving them mastery over their environment. A child who is comfortable walking around her neighbourhood negotiating busy streets and roads is no longer dependent on her parents.

She is able to visit her friends, go to after school leisure activities, and go to shops on her own. The world suddenly opens up to her, giving her a type of freedom that's unavailable when she has to rely on others for transport. These feelings of mastery are important as it helps her feel a great sense of control. She is no longer at the beck and call of her parents. But this greater freedom also involves an element of risk. Suddenly the world becomes a little unpredictable. Things may go wrong. She may take a wrong turn one day and lose her way. She may encounter people whom she wouldn't normally meet who make her feel uncomfortable. She may simply experience the extreme elements of wind, rain or heat and have to cope with these. She may have to deal with uncertainty or situations such as losing her way that make her a little fearful. Each time she does so successfully she gets an important lesson about resilience and builds on her feelings of mastery and control.

"Anxiety takes a back seat when kids face real fears albeit in relatively safe, confined environments."

Anxiety takes a back seat when kids face real fears, albeit in relatively safe, confined environments. The experience of fending for yourself is invaluable, as it not only builds kids problem-solving skillsets and their resourcefulness but it gives them the confidence they need to successfully negotiate future difficulties and, in doing so, overcome their fears.

Making anxiety normal

The term anxiety is value laden. There is still the perception that something is lacking in a person if they experience anxiety. The fact is, we all experience anxiety from time to time. It's a normal emotion, which can help us to perform at our best. However, when it lingers longer than it should or pops up when we least expect it, then anxiety doesn't serve us well. As a community, we have a lot to learn about anxiety, what it looks like, how it impacts on our lives and also how we can manage it effectively. The greatest challenge for the current generation of adults is to not only normalise anxiety, but to learn the skills and tools to manage anxiety effectively, so that future generations won't have to ask the question, "Why is my child so anxious?" Skilling up future generations to manage their mental states effectively is the best legacy that the parents of today can leave.

* Many thanks to my colleague Dr Jodi Richardson for her contribution to this chapter, and her ongoing efforts to positively impact families, schools and children who are touched by epidemic of anxiety.

Anxiety can be debilitating but there is so much parents and teachers can do to help kids when they are anxious. Join Michael Grose and Dr Jodi Richardson in their ground-breaking Parenting Anxious Kids Online Course, where you'll learn a variety of tools to help manage and respond to anxiety both in the moment and over the long term. Learn more at parentingideas.com.au

Hugh van Cuylenburg

Hugh van Cuylenburg has been working in education for over 15 years, teaching both primary and secondary in a range of educational settings. The highlight of his teaching career was the year he spent in the far north of India volunteering and living at an underprivileged school in the Himalayas. It was here that he discovered resilience in its purest form.

Inspired by this experience Hugh returned to Melbourne and commenced working on his own program for schools. 'The Resilience Project' was born. Having completed his post graduate studies, looking at resilience and wellbeing, Hugh has developed and facilitated programs for over 650 schools Australia wide. In 2015, the National Rugby League asked Hugh to run workshops at every single club in the competition. Since then, he has worked with the Australian Cricket Team, the Australian Netball Team, the Australian Women's Soccer Team, The Jillaroos and a number of AFL teams. Beyond the team environment, Hugh has been lucky enough to work one on one with individuals such as Steve Smith, Dustin Martin and Billy Slater.

Outside of schools and sport, Hugh has presented to over 200 corporate groups as a keynote speaker, where he teaches the same principles as he does when he is working with the prep kids in schools across the country.

His favourite past time is spending time with his partner Penny and their one year old son, Benji.

www.theresilienceproject.com.au

The Resilience Project

@ResilienceP

Discovering resilience

Where it all began

Of all the meals my family shared together, dinner was the most painful. The inevitable arguments, the tearful, exasperated rebuttals. They would always concern the food left untouched on my sister's plate.

My sister would try desperately to explain why the food was best left uneaten. My mum would respond in turn, tears welling in her eyes.

Dinner time was difficult for us all. That is, until my little sister Georgia was admitted to hospital. At 17 years of age, she had dropped to crisis weight. Although not an overly short person, Georgia had managed to drop to approximately 30 kilograms. There was nothing of her. Anorexia Nervosa had absolutely ravaged my little sister. In fact, it hadn't just ravaged my little sister, but our whole family.

Fast forward a few years. I found myself living in the far north of India, in a desert community in the Himalayas. To describe it as a life-changing experience is an understatement. In this desert community there was no running water, no electricity and no beds. We slept on the floor. I was there volunteering as a primary school teacher in the local school.

I clearly remember meeting a young boy by the name of Stunzin on my first day at the school. Never before had a person's happiness and joy made such a great impression on me. I couldn't quite believe it. I would often find myself getting the giggles when in his company, as his happiness and positivity were just so infectious.

My stint in the community, living at the principal's house, was only ever meant to last a couple of weeks. On what was meant to be my last night in the village community, I remember lying on the floor and having a startling realisation. I thought, "I'm not sure I've ever felt this happy before."

Now, I'm lucky because I'm naturally a very happy person, but I recall thinking that something felt different. I was so calm, and so full of joy. For two weeks, I hadn't had access to any electrical devices. I hadn't been on the internet or had a shower; yet here I was, lying on the floor, full of joy. I decided to go for a walk through the village to soak up this extraordinary atmosphere one last time. It was on this walk that my life changed forever. To cut a long story short, I came across little Stunzin, and I was at once confronted by his living circumstances. He slept on a dirt floor, under a very simple structure that acted as shelter. That's all he had. The happiest person I have ever met had very little, if anything, to call his own.

I didn't sleep a wink that night, I couldn't stop thinking about my little sister Georgia. How was this possible? Georgia grew up in a leafy suburb in Melbourne, with a loving family and a beautiful home. She had everything she had ever wanted growing up. Yet my sister, like so many people here in Australia, found it hard to be happy. She, like many others, was suffering from mental illness.

At that point, I remember thinking, "I'm not leaving." I decided to stay for as long as it would take to work out what the people in this community did every day that made them so happy. Because the more I thought about it, I realised that it wasn't just Stunzin, but the whole community. These people were just so happy.

> **"G.E.M –
> Gratitude,
> Empathy and
> Mindfulness"**

I stayed for nearly four months in this community, and I saw three things that its people did every single day. Conveniently, there is a lovely, easy-to-remember acronym for them: G.E.M – Gratitude, Empathy and Mindfulness. This chapter of the book will focus on these practices. It will explain how you can apply them, and how your life will change as a result. At least 30 years of research has demonstrated that practising G.E.M will allow us to be happier, experience better mental health, and be more resilient.

Gratitude

I will try to steer away from a dictionary definition here. Gratitude is when you pay attention to what you have, and not worry about the things that you don't have. So many people in Australia live by a model of happiness called the 'if and then' model. If I buy this car, then I will feel happy. If we buy this house, then we will feel happy. If I get these marks at school, then I will feel happy. There is nothing wrong with aspiring towards these things, but we just can't pin our happiness on them. Why? Because months down the track, even they won't satiate our desires.

Gratitude is when you pay attention to what you already have.

"Gratitude is when you pay attention to what you already have."

On my first day teaching in this village community, I remember a group of boys excitedly taking me by the hand and asking me to come and see their playground. We arrived at the playground minutes later, whereupon they stood in front of the equipment and pointed over their shoulders. I didn't look at their faces. I just looked at the equipment. The swings were completely broken, and the see-saw was rusted. I assumed they were saying, "Hey, sir, look how bad this is." Then I looked at their faces and realised they were actually saying, "Hey, sir! CHECK THIS OUT!" They loved their play equipment. Why? Because they were very good at paying attention to what they had. You couldn't get near the play equipment at lunch time; there were kids swarming all over it.

So, how do you start paying attention to the good things that surround you? You practise gratitude. How do you practise gratitude? It's simple. Very simple, in fact. You simply record three things that went well for you every day. It doesn't matter how you do it, but here are some suggestions:

- Write them in a note pad beside your bed.

- Write them on the shower screen door (using your finger, in the steam – not with a Texta as you walk past your shower screen!)

- Have a group discussion around the dinner table with all family members and talk what went well for them during the day.

- Download The Resilience Project app on your phone to record three things that went well for you (shameless plug #1).

Please note, the question is NOT, "What are three things you are grateful for?" This is a limited, and to be quite honest, boring thing to do. You will end up repeating yourself, as we tend to only recall the big, tangible things in our lives. Asking yourself, "What went well today?" gives you access to the unique, enjoyable moments of your day.

> *"Gratitude is a simple practice which has a big impact on such a complex condition – our mental health."*

According to the research, what happens to you as a result of practising gratitude is extraordinary. By its very nature, this activity positions you to scan your world for the good stuff. This makes us experience more positive emotions. Beyond this, it has many other benefits. It helps us to sleep better, improves our immune system, and after months of practice, actually reduces anxiety and depression. In one study, it was actually found that the practice of gratitude reduces suicidal ideation. This is what I love about gratitude: it is a simple practice which has a big impact on such a complex condition – our mental health.

Empathy

Empathy is when you feel what someone else feels. It's when you put yourself in someone else's shoes. The more empathetic you are, the more likely you are to act in a kind manner. The neuroscience behind kindness is incredible. When we do something kind for someone, our brain releases a hormone called oxytocin. Oxytocin is known as the 'love hormone'. It is the happiness hormone. This is not an underpinning reason for why we do things for other people (to make ourselves feel good) but it is proof that as a species, we are hard-wired to be kind. We are rewarded for kindness.

On my first day in the school in India, I did the most embarrassing thing as I walked into the classroom full of eager and curious Grade Threes. Such was my enthusiasm and anxiety, I didn't realise that the doorway only came up to my forehead. As I marched into the classroom, I smashed my head on the mud brick doorway. I've never seen Grade Threes laugh so much in my entire life. I remember stooping over, checking to see if I had drawn blood. I said, "Guys, I've really hurt my head." They said, "Yes, it's very funny."

The next day, as I walked a little more tentatively towards the classroom, I saw Stunzin standing at the threshold. He was pointing at the doorway with a grin on his face. "What are you laughing at?" I inquired. "Have a look, sir." He had found an old rag. I don't know where he found it, but he had filled it with leaves and sand and wrapped it around the doorway to create padding. I was blown away. "Yesterday looked bad, sir."

This kid was always looking out for opportunities to be kind to other people. Whether it was finding other students who looked lonely in the playground, dropping in on students who had missed school because they were unwell, or offering up genuine and authentic compliments, he was instinctively kind. This is one of the reasons that he was so happy.

Here are some tips on how to encourage kindness either in your own life or perhaps in your kids:

- Try to perform a random act of kindness each week.

- Have a think about your friends and family. Do you know of anyone who is doing it tough at the moment? If so, reach out to them. Perhaps plan this as a family. Ask your kids the question, "What could we do to be kind to this person?" Get your kids to carry out the act of kindness.

"Try to perform a random act of kindness each week."

- *Model the correct behaviour in front of your kids.* By this, I mean: let people into traffic, hold the door open for someone, give people authentic compliments, shout someone a coffee, and treat your partner in the way that you want your children to be treated when they grow up. Modelling the correct behaviour is the most powerful way to influence your child.

Mindfulness

Mindfulness is the ability to be calm and present. A mindful person has control over what they are focusing on. As a society, we are not mindful. Are we calm? Not even close. The most common mental illness in Australia right now is anxiety disorder. Are we calm in Australia? The next time you make a small mistake whilst driving your car, have a look at how people respond around you. Beeping horns, glares and stares. We are so on edge here in Australia. Are we present? The research shows that we spend 49% of our waking time thinking about the future. And these wretched devices that we are so addicted to are doing nothing but exacerbating the problem.

"Mindfulness is the ability to be calm and present."

Everyday, from 8.30 to 9.00am, the kids at the desert school in India practised meditation. At first, I thought they were saying their prayers, until it was explained to me that the kids were doing their daily mindfulness. This was 10 years ago. I clearly remember thinking to myself, "What a ridiculous waste of time!" That is, until I joined in. Two weeks later, I remember walking to the school when I caught myself thinking, "Oh, yes, I can't wait for meditation today."

I need to be very clear here – I am not a mindfulness expert. If fact, mindfulness has been an ongoing challenge for me over the past decade. I do, however, have a huge amount of experience at introducing this practice into people's lives – people who you would think traditionally would be quite opposed to meditation. It is not necessarily sitting still in a ridiculously flexible yogic pose, hands raised to the air (although this is a great way to go about it). I have tried many ways over the journey. As a starting point, there are some fantastic apps out there that can introduce you to the practice of meditation. Try the apps below and see what work best for you.

- The Resilience Project (shameless plug #2)
- Headspace
- Insight Timer
- Calm

Just 10 minutes a day will give you a calmer and more present disposition as you navigate the ups and downs of your day. I have moved away from sitting meditation myself. I am a very active, hands-on person, so I have introduced this into my meditation style. In my late 30s, I have started training for Masters Athletics. A ridiculous pursuit really, but one that I am enjoying enormously. Having played cricket and football since I could walk, my body is riddled with injuries, aches and pains. I am training for the 200- and 400-metre sprint. My warm-up has become my new daily mindfulness activity.

> *"Just 10 minutes a day will give you a calmer and more present disposition as you navigate the ups and downs of your day."*

It is a 30-minute process which involves slowly and deliberately warming up every muscle in the body. All I think about during the 30 minutes is how my body is feeling. That's it. I progress from a stiff and sore hobble, to half an hour later, a supple, loose and dynamic* sprint. My mind has had a rest, as all it has done for 30 minutes is focus its attention on what is happening right here and now.

My sister's recovery

I am very happy to say that my sister Georgia no longer suffers from poor mental health. Why? Every day, my sister writes down the three things that went well for her. Every day, my sister meditates. Every day, my sister performs an act of kindness for someone. My sister battled with mental illness for many years. Mum and Dad sent her to every specialist under the sun. Nothing quite seemed to work. G.E.M, however, has become a big part of her life and a significant factor in her recovery. I am not saying that G.E.M is the sliver bullet that instantly heals everyone, but what it does is very powerful. It gradually pushes us up the mental health spectrum. Our mental health is like anything else in life: if we want to be good at something, we have to practise. My sister practises her mental health every day, and I cannot begin to tell you how proud I am of her.

*There is absolutely nothing dynamic about my sprinting style, no matter how warmed up I am!

Sharon Witt

Sharon Witt has been immersed in teen world for over two decades in her role as a secondary teacher, author, and presenter to adolescents and their parents around the country.

She is a regular media commentator on issues impacting young people, parenting and educational issues. Sharon often appears regularly on television, as well as having weekly parenting segments on radio. She also writes for a number of publications including *Mici*, *Gigi* and *Bella-Rae* magazines for adolescent girls.

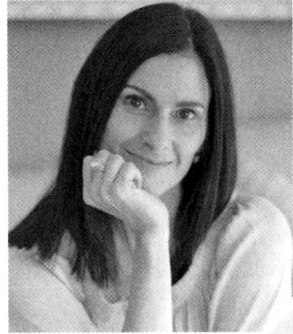

In 2016, Sharon launched the Resilient Kids Conference for parents and educators. What began as a small event in Melbourne has now grown into a nationwide and soon-to-be international event, providing education, encouragement and resources to those who work with children and teens.

Sharon is the author of 12 books, written for young people to help guide them through many of the issues they face in early years, including the best-selling *Teen Talk*, *Girlwise* and *Wiseguys* series. Her ten-week resilience curriculum programs, 'Girlwise' and 'Wiseguys', are used in primary schools throughout Australia.

www.sharonwitt.com.au

Sharon Witt

sharonwittauthor

@sharon_witt

Raising resilient parents

Resilience is a term that has gained traction in recent years, becoming the "buzzword" if you will. It's easy to see why it's a word that resonates with parents, as we all have similar goals – namely, to develop strong, capable, well-balanced and above all, kind and decent young people.

Many parents seem to be struggling with the basics of raising children, and they are desperate for any guidance or support on offer. However, as a professional who works with children and parents on a regular basis, what I have discovered is that many are operating in survival mode.

Parents are endeavouring to raise resilient children, yet they are floundering under the immense pressures of life, and its myriad physical, emotional and mental health challenges.

I have heard the same refrain far too often from exasperated educators lately… "Forget the kids; we need to help the *parents* develop resilience!"

Indeed, if one or more parents are struggling with managing life and their own resilience, how can we expect our children and teenagers to follow suit?

Throughout this book, a number of incredible experts have touched on some of the biggest and most important influences on young people today – including cyber safety, pornography and bullying – and they offer strategies to help our kids navigate this minefield and raise them to become confident, resilient people.

However, this journey really starts with us as parents. I truly believe that raising resilient parents is absolutely essential, if we want to raise resilient kids. This chapter therefore aims to provide parents with a backpack of encouragement and strategies to develop their own resilience skill set, which will in turn, help us to become stronger and more resilient parents.

In a nutshell, we need to model resilience for our children. We can do this in a variety of ways, and it will be different for every person and family; however, the aim of the game is to get the foundation right. This is so important because the reality is, our kids are going to be more influenced by what we *do* than what we *say*. It's much more powerful to demonstrate resilience to them in our own decisions, behaviours and habits, rather than simply instructing them on how to overcome their own challenges.

> *"We need to model resilience for our children."*

Resilience rule book

The role of parent does not come with a rule book. It would be ideal if, during one of your first few dates as a new couple, you turned the discussion to what sort of parent you want to be, what values you want to instill in any children you might produce together, and how you will both manage the load to survive the distance. It's not exactly sexy, but it would certainly save a lot of heartbreak!

Here's what really happens…

We usually spend the first six or more weeks post-birth in some sort of sleep-deprived haze, often battling through by trial and error. Then, most of us spend the next few years 'winging it'.

It's not until we are knee-deep in the trenches of parenting that we work out what we are doing and how to parent well. Somehow along the way, however, many parents forget about their own health and wellbeing.

We all want to raise capable and resilient young people. The reality is, however, that the more we invest in our children in this ever-complex world (which is increasingly over stimulated and highly scheduled), the more we as parents are stretched to capacity.

And this is happening in homes where parents are already stretched by their own careers and work obligations. We are seeing increased numbers of parents working outside of the home. According to the Australian Bureau of Statistics, some 64 per cent of families have both parents in the workplace, with 25 per cent having both parents holding down full-time employment.

There's nothing wrong with being a working parent, but when we're in this situation, it requires a little more attention to ensure the whole family is not just surviving, but thriving. If we want to raise resilient and well-rounded young people, it stands to reason that we would need to begin by ensuring that the primary carers are taken care of, too.

When parents and carers invest in taking care of themselves and their family environment, they put in place protective factors that reduce the risk of developing mental health concerns.

Think about it this way: when travelling by air with children, safety instructions are always given by airline staff for parents to first use the oxygen masks on themselves *before* they administer it to their child.

Parents and carers would benefit from remembering this basic instruction in all areas of life. To look after our kids and be optimal parents, raising children who have the tools and skills they need to prosper, we need to start by modelling these very traits to them from the outset.

So how do we begin the process of building our own resilience as parents?

"... we would need to begin with making sure the primary carers are taken care of, too."

As I've already touched on, our kids are going to be more influenced by what we do than what we say. Here, I'm going to share some of the main strategies that I believe will help to raise resilient parents:

Demonstrate self-care

Our children see us build our own resilience when they observe us looking after ourselves. We can't be the best, strongest, healthiest, most vital versions of ourselves if we're not taking care of ourselves.

In my own situation, my children can see me focus on my exercise. They see me eating well, they observe how I handle my friendships, and they watch how I proactively give myself time out. All of these little acts of self-care help me to fortify myself and ensure I'm ready to cope if, and when, challenging situations arise.

It may seem selfish, but it's actually selfless – as it's demonstrating what self-care and resilience looks like. It's becoming even more important to model self-care in today's fast-paced world: our kids are often over-scheduled, and we can easily fall into that trap ourselves, too. We need to model for our kids what it looks like to have down time.

"It's becoming even more important to model self-care in today's fast-paced world."

This could include: booking a night away at a hotel by yourself or pitching a tent in a caravan park an hour away; planning a night out with your friends; arranging for your kids to have a sleepover so you can have a night of Netflix on the couch and a sleep-in the next day. It's all about taking that time to retreat from the pressures of everyday life, even if only for a few hours, and replenish yourself.

Personally, one of the things I do is spend a week at a hotel by myself every year. I've gone to the same hotel for the last 20 years, and every year I return there to give myself seven days off of my life. It's seven days spent 'off the grid', where I can go to bed when I want to; eat what I want, where I want, when I want; choose how I want to spend my days; and ultimately just switch off. Because my life is so busy, and I give so much of my energy to everyone else as a parent, teacher, educator and speaker, this time that I spend investing in myself and my own wellbeing is essential. I have to fuel myself – because you can't pour from an empty cup!

Take care of you

This is quite similar to my first point, though I want to take it one step further. That first point was about prioritising our own self-care and ensuring we're not the last person being looked after. Now, I want to suggest that we proactively monitor and manage our own health when difficult situations arise.

In the midst of being a parent, you are of no value to your kids if you fall apart and can't climb your way back on top of things. When you get hit with something difficult, you may fall apart temporarily and mope in bed for the day – but your kids then need to see you get back up again. If you find that you can't resurface, that's okay; but it means that you need to get help. It's our job as parents, to model for our kids that it's okay to reach out for support when we need it.

I have recently been through a traumatic event, and soon afterwards, I booked in to see a psychologist. I told my children what I was doing and explained, "There's nothing wrong with me, and there's nothing wrong with reaching out for help. This has been difficult, and I need some guidance."

I think about it this way: if our car is running poorly, we see a mechanic. If we have a toothache, we visit the dentist. So, if we're struggling with challenging circumstances and we're not sure how to navigate the way forward, then it's a good idea to see a therapist or psychologist to gain valuable insight and helpful strategies.

Be honest and upfront

As parents, we obviously want to shield our kids from trauma. However, it can be so beneficial to their wellbeing if we are open, honest and transparent. When we experienced a traumatic event a few years ago, I called my dear friend Michael Carr-Gregg and said, "I don't know what to do or how to help my kids to process this… help!".

He suggested that I tell my 16-year-old son *everything*. "What he can imagine is going on is far worse that the truth," Michael advised. "Tell him everything about what has happened so far, and what the plan is going forward."

It went against every fibre of my being to follow his advice; I wanted to protect my son from the situation, not expand his involvement in it. But do you know what? He handled it so well. Being upfront with him and giving him the space to ask questions helped him to gain some control and perspective.

A little while ago, someone I know received a cancer diagnosis. She asked me for some tips on how to manage the situation with her teenage children. I said, "Listen, I'm no psychologist, but the best one I know advised me to be upfront in these situations. It went against everything I thought I wanted to do when handling difficult situations with my kids, but if you tell them everything you know and keep them involved, it may be better than allowing the kids to fill in the blanks on their own." My friend followed this advice and later told me that her teenagers handled everything so much better than she expected. Happily, I can also report that she's in remission now.

Develop your tribe

They don't say that parenting takes a village for no reason! Parenting is a team sport, and by expanding our own network of trusted friends and relatives, it makes the process of raising children much less isolating and lonely.

Having a tribe is about sharing experiences. When we share, it gives other people the permission to say… *me too!* There is so much relief and growth in these types of shared conversations and experiences. We're often scared about sharing, but when we do lean on people and share our story, we're opening the door for them to share their stories, too.

"When we do lean on people and share our story, we're opening the door for them to share their stories, too."

You're not doing this parenting caper on your own, even though it may sometimes feel like it. And if it *does* feel that way, or if you feel like you *don't* have a tribe, you might have to step out and look for it and develop your own support system.

For some people, that may be on social media, especially if you're in a remote area or you can't or don't like getting out and about. You can join groups that gather to discuss specific concerns, like anxiety support, parenting forums, having children with special needs, or to do with sports or hobbies.

A mother's group can also be really helpful if you're a new parent, and going to parenting events and gatherings can be a great place to connect with like-minded souls. Turn up to parent nights at school. Even though they can be a pain in the backside, you will find there are many other parents going through the same issues you're going through with your kids, and sharing the experiences could result in you learning fresh ideas and new solutions.

You could also join a local interest group, to do with sports, hobbies or exercise group – something that gets you out and meeting people. If you already have friends in your life, then find ways to nourish those relationships. As I often tell kids, in order to make a friend, you need to be one first. Practice being friendly, step out of your comfort zone a little bit and start a conversation; even if it feels hard at first, the benefits will more than make up for it.

Maintain perspective

This is all about modelling resilience, no matter what happens. Even in the darkest of hours when the most difficult things happen, we can model to our children the ability to not only survive, but to eventually thrive again.

One of the most effective ways of building our own resilience is to maintain a sense of perspective. We can often catastrophise things; if a glass breaks, we fly off the handle. To maintain perspective is to have the attitude of: well, at least it wasn't your arm that broke. There are worse things that could happen.

A little while after my son got his license, I let him borrow my car. He'd parked in a normal car park, in a well-lit street, but when he returned to the car at 10pm, he noticed scuff marks on the bonnet. Then, he noticed the beer bottles scattered around the ground.

It turned out that a group of drunk people had jumped all over the car, leaving massive dints everywhere on the bonnet and roof. He rang me, very distressed about what had happened. I replied, "Buddy, just hop in the car and drive home. You're safe, which is the main thing. The car is insured and this can all be fixed."

When he came home, he was devastated. He felt responsible, and I reiterated to him that it's just my car, and panels could be fixed; it would be much worse if you had come back to the car, and the drunks were still there. They did something like $10k worth of damage, but it was all repaired. Most importantly, hopefully my son was able to learn how to maintain perspective himself, and draw on this in the future.

Set and maintain boundaries

I often say yes first, before even properly thinking about it. Can you help with this project? Appear on this panel? Give a talk at this event? Help my kids with this problem?

Whatever the question or request, I often say yes, and then work out how I'm going to make it happen. Whilst this kind of approach can serve us well when we're building our careers, it can also eventually lead to burnout. When we push ourselves to the enth degree and give and give of ourselves, we can be left with nothing but a burnt-out shell.

This is why learning to set boundaries is absolutely crucial. The ability to say "no" is a learned skill and something we need to practice for our own self-preservation. It doesn't even have to be a "no"; it could be a "not now".

"Building boundaries is important in our own lives, and they're just as important in our children's' lives."

I am terrible with saying no, which is why I have now enlisted a PA to help control my diary and manage my time more effectively. If I am planning to attend a conference, she now schedules in downtime before and after events, so I can properly prepare and debrief. In the past, I would have squeezed in extra obligations, meetings, catch ups and appointments, but she will now draw a firm line in the sand to say: "Sharon is booked up then, but how about the next week?"

Building boundaries is important in our own lives, and they're just as important in our children's' lives. Learning to be patient and to compromise are traits that contribute towards resilience. We can't give our kids what they want all day, every day, or they'll never be able to adapt and respond appropriately when things don't go their way.

From the smaller discussions ("No, we can't go to the movies this weekend as we're busy, but we can look at going next weekend") to the bigger decisions ("It's too expensive for you to do so many after-school activities, so you need to choose your favourite one"), helping your kids to understand and respond to boundaries will set them up with the right framework to develop resilience.

Show our kids that it's okay to fail

An essential skill that all parents should aim to teach our kids, is to demonstrate that it's okay to fail. This is an opportunity to show them *how* we bounce back.

"The truth is, nobody has got it all together, all the time..."

Throughout their life, our young people are not going to achieve every goal they set for themselves. They're going to make mistakes or take a different path, and they're going to feel disappointed when things don't turn out how they expected them to. This is life!

We shouldn't sweep these feelings under the carpet or encourage our kids to simply keep their chin up and look for the next goal to aim for. Instead, we should give them the tools they need to move through failure and disappointment, knowing that a) these feelings won't last; and b) it's okay to not be okay sometimes.

The truth is, nobody has got it all together, all the time (even though social media might skew this reality somewhat!)

Moreover, while it's okay to not be okay, it's not okay to stay in that trench. Wallow, sulk and have your moment of not coping… and then learn how to pick yourself up again, using some of the strategies I've outlined in this chapter.

I can recall my own moment of not being okay. I was on holidays at the beach, having just survived a very difficult year that included going through a divorce.

I wasn't okay.

I wrote a brief post on social media, where I shared, "I'm not okay, but I will be. I feel like I'm overwhelmed, that I'm only just paddling above water, and

I feel like I've let people down. But I know this is just a season, and it will pass."

After sharing and opening up that vulnerable side of myself, I received around a dozen private messages from friends and colleagues who were in the same boat. One confessed that she'd just had a baby and wasn't coping; others were struggling with grief, job loss and relationship breakdowns. "I'm not okay either, and I want to get help, but I don't know where to start," they wrote.

Though I didn't have all the answers for them, we shared some conversations and got the ball rolling on some ideas and solutions to help them dig themselves out of their trenches. This is the value of having a tribe.

Keep your sense of humour

At the end of the day, you have to keep your sense of humour! Never take yourself too seriously. Yes, my children think I'm an embarrassment when I act like a dork or do silly things. But you have to laugh and seek out the funny side of life. After all, none of us are getting out of it alive.